NEW VANGUARD • 187

# IMPERIAL JAPANESE NAVY LIGHT CRUISERS 1941–45

**MARK STILLE**                ILLUSTRATED BY PAUL WRIGHT

First published in Great Britain in 2011 by Osprey Publishing,
Midland House, West Way, Botley, Oxford, OX2 0PH, UK
44–02 23rd St, Suite 219, Long Island City, NY 11101, USA

E-mail: info@ospreypublishing.com

Osprey Publishing is part of the Osprey Group

A CIP catalog record for this book is available from the British Library

Print ISBN: 978 1 84908 562 5
PDF e-book ISBN: 978 1 84908 563 2
EPUB e-book ISBN: 978 1 78096 040 1

Page layout by: Melissa Orrom Swan, Oxford
Index by Michael Parkin
Typeset in Sabon and Myriad Pro
Originated by PDQ Digital Media Solutions, Suffolk
Printed in China through Worldprint Ltd

12 13 14 15 16   10 9 8 7 6 5 4 3 2 1

Osprey Publishing is supporting the Woodland Trust, the UK's leading
woodland conservation charity, by funding the dedication of trees.

**www.ospreypublishing.com**

## ACKNOWLEDGEMENTS

The author would like to thank the staffs of the Naval History and Heritage
Command Photographic Section, the Yamato Museum, and Tohru Kizu,
editor of *Ships of the World* magazine for their assistance in procuring
photographs used in this book. Keith Allen also provided a valuable review
of the text.

## DEDICATION

This book is dedicated to Fred Wilson, veteran of the Pacific War.

# CONTENTS

# IMPERIAL JAPANESE NAVY LIGHT CRUISERS 1941–45

## INTRODUCTION

The Imperial Navy went to war with 17 light cruisers and another three cruiser-sized training ships. Of these, most were 5,500-ton ships designed to act as destroyer squadron flagships. This made the Imperial Navy's light cruisers much different than their American counterparts. During the war, the Japanese built another five cruisers, all but one of which maintained the basic design premise of being able to act as a flagship for the Imperial Navy's destroyers. Because these ships served in a supporting role, they have not received much attention. This book tells the story of the 25 light cruisers that served the Imperial Navy during World War II.

## JAPANESE LIGHT CRUISER DEVELOPMENT

The first cruiser class designed entirely by the Japanese was the four-ship Tone class, of which the lead ship was completed in 1910. These were also the last piston-engine Japanese cruisers. They were followed by the three-ship Chikuma class. These ships were equipped with turbine engines and a larger 6-inch gun main armament. Both of these classes of protected cruisers (typed as second-class cruisers by the Japanese) were designed to act as scouts for the battle fleet.

After the outbreak of World War I, the Navy Ministry presented its plan to augment the fleet. This was approved in a modified form by the Imperial Diet in 1916. Included in this plan, known as the New Naval Construction Program of 1916, were funds for two light cruisers. These two ships were projected to be only 3,500 tons – smaller than the earlier scout cruisers – and were designed to be flotilla leaders for the Imperial Navy's growing number of modern destroyers.

Naval competition with the United States began to take shape as early as 1916. This led to the approval of the 8-4 Fleet Completion Program, which was enacted in July 1917. Originally this program included nine cruisers, six improved 3,500-ton ships, and three larger 7,200-ton scout cruisers. By 1917 it was obvious that the 3,500-ton cruisers were inadequate to act as squadron leaders for the current generation of Japanese destroyers and that they did not compare favorably with foreign counterparts. Plans for more of these were scrapped, and a 5,500-ton cruiser design was adopted. Eight of these were funded in 1917 with the ninth ship converted to an experimental ship. In 1918, another three 5,500-ton cruisers were funded.

Four more 5,500-ton ships were approved as part of the 1920 8-8 Fleet Completion Program, though the last unit was quickly cancelled. Concurrent with the funding of the series of 5,500-ton cruisers was a series of studies devoted to developing a suitable design for a large scout cruiser. The 5,500-ton design was a deadend as the basis for a larger scout cruiser. The 5,500-ton cruisers featured a main battery of seven 5.5-inch guns, all in single mounts and only six of which could fire broadside. In comparison, both the American and British navies had also decided to design and build large scout cruisers. In the case of the Americans, this was the 7,500-ton Omaha class with twelve 6-inch guns with a much heavier broadside. The British designed a similar ship, the 9,750-ton Hawkins class with seven 7.5-inch guns. In response, by 1922 the Japanese settled on a 7,500-ton large cruiser design (see New Vanguard 176, *Imperial Japanese Navy Heavy Cruisers* for details).

By the time the Washington Naval Treaty was signed on February 6, 1922, the size and composition of the Imperial Navy's light cruiser force was already set. The Washington Treaty capped construction of capital ships and also had a dramatic effect on the Imperial Navy's cruiser force. Despite the fact that the treaty did not restrict the numbers of cruisers that could be built, it did change the course of Japanese cruiser construction. The only limit placed on cruisers was in maximum tonnage (10,000 tons) and the size of the main battery (8-inch). Since capital ship construction was capped, all major navies began a cruiser-building spree. For both the Americans and Japanese, the new 10,000-ton limit was the baseline for subsequent designs. The 5,500-ton design was not further developed.

The London Naval Treaty was signed in April 1930 and this agreement limited cruiser tonnage for all signatories. The Japanese allotments were 108,400 tons (standard) for cruisers with guns bigger than 6.1 inch, and 100,450 tons for ships with guns up to 6.1 inches. The Japanese had built up to their limits in the first (heavy cruiser) category, but only had 98,415 tons on the books for light cruisers. Through retirement of old units and allowances to replace aging units, the Imperial Navy assembled 50,955 tons to use for construction of new light cruisers. It was decided that this allotment would be used to build four 8,500-ton ships by 1936, followed by two 8,450-ton units. These were heavily armed and well-protected ships, which became the

Mogami class and the Tone class, respectively. The four Mogamis were built and armed with 6.1-inch guns, but were later converted into heavy cruisers after the Japanese withdrew from the London Treaty. The Tone class was completed as heavy cruisers. This was the missing generation of Japanese light cruisers. When the Japanese again planned to build light cruisers, they returned to the destroyer flagship model. Meanwhile, since the London Treaty restricted the number of cruisers that could be built, the 5,500-ton ships underwent modernization in the 1930s. The Imperial Navy went to war with 17 light cruisers, 14 of which were the 5,500-ton design.

## JAPANESE NAVAL STRATEGY AND THE ROLE OF THE LIGHT CRUISER

Between the wars, the Imperial Navy attempted to devise weapons and tactics to negate its numerical inferiority to the U.S. Navy. Japanese naval strategists assumed that the American fleet would advance into the western Pacific in any conflict, and it was there that the Japanese planned to fight a decisive battle in the mold of Tsushima to destroy the Americans. The decisive battle concept was built around a carefully choreographed action in which the Imperial Navy's torpedo attack forces would severely weaken the U.S. battle fleet in a night engagement before the ultimate clash of battle lines. In this scenario, the Japanese Night Battle Force would subject the American fleet to a heavy barrage of long-range Type 93 oxygen-propelled torpedoes. The nucleus of the force was the four fast battleships of the Kongo class and the four Takao-class heavy cruisers. These would open a path through the defensive ring of the American fleet, allowing the special squadron of three modified Kuma-class torpedo cruisers, each with a broadside of 20 torpedoes, and the destroyer squadrons, led by 5,500-ton cruisers, to deliver massed and devastating torpedo attacks.

## JAPANESE LIGHT CRUISER TACTICS

Japanese light cruisers were designed as flagships for destroyer squadrons. Organizationally, a destroyer squadron was comprised of three or four destroyer divisions, each ideally with four destroyers. These destroyer squadrons were key components of the Imperial Navy's plan to defeat the U.S. Navy. The light cruisers were required to provide accommodations for the admiral leading the destroyer squadron and his staff. The extra space offered by a light cruiser was required to exercise proper command and control of the squadron. This included expanded space for the staff and additional communications gear. Light cruiser bridges incorporated an operations or combat room. This was nothing more than a space containing a conference table with chairs where future operations were planned or which was used by the staff as a command center. In no way was it similar to the concept of a combat information center later developed by the Americans.

The light cruisers had a tactical role in the massed torpedo attacks planned by the Imperial Navy as a

This excellent starboard quarter view of *Oi* shows it in June 1937 before it was taken into the yards for conversion into a torpedo cruiser. The layout of the main armament is clearly shown. (Naval History and Heritage Command)

centerpiece of its decisive battle concept. These ships were tasked to lead the attack of the destroyer squadrons. With their heavier firepower, they were to protect the attacking destroyers from gunfire from enemy destroyers and cruisers. Though Japanese light cruisers were equipped with a comparatively light torpedo armament, these also would contribute to any massed torpedo attack.

*Sendai* in 1939 acting as a destroyer squadron leader. An unidentified destroyer is on its starboard beam and a Hatsuhara-class destroyer is steaming off its starboard quarter. (Yamato Museum)

There were many more light cruisers built than existing destroyer squadrons and the excess were also formed into cruiser divisions. These had several missions. Some were directly attached to the main battle fleet in order to provide protection for the battleships and also to conduct long-range patrols and searches for enemy forces. A secondary mission was to provide protection for trade routes.

## JAPANESE LIGHT CRUISER WEAPONS

### Main Guns

The main battery of Japanese light cruisers did not compare favorably to their foreign counterparts. While the Americans and British opted for a 6-inch main gun for their light cruisers being built in the 1920s, the Japanese settled for a 5.5-inch weapon. Additionally, Japanese ships carried fewer of these smaller guns compared to the American scout cruisers of the period. The 5.5-inch gun selected by the Japanese dated from 1914 and was already in service as the secondary gun on two classes of battleships. It was hand-operated, so possessed a relatively low rate of fire, and the range was inferior to the American 6-inch gun, but it compared favorably to the British gun of the same caliber. In general, Japanese light cruisers were less well armed than their foreign counterparts, and this trend continued when the Japanese designed two new classes of light cruisers in the late 1930s.

| Japanese Light Cruiser Main Guns | | | | |
|---|---|---|---|---|
| Type | Class | Max. Elevation (degrees) | Max. Range (yards) | Rate of Fire (rounds/minute) |
| Type 3 5.5 inch/50 caliber | Tenryu | 20 | 17,220 | 6–10 |
| Type 3 5.5 inch/50 caliber | Kuma, Nagara | 25 | 19,080 | 6–10 |
| Type 3 5.5 inch/50 caliber | Sendai, Yubari | 30 | 20,820 | 6–10 |
| Type 3 5.5 inch/50 caliber | Katori | 35 | 21,600 | 6–10 |
| Type 41 6 inch/50 caliber | Agano | 45 | 22,890 | 6 |
| Type 3 6.1 inch/60 caliber | Oyodo | 45 | 29,865 | 5 |

### Torpedo Armament

The actual main battery of the Imperial Navy's light cruisers was their torpedo armament. Given the primary mission of Japanese light cruisers, a heavy torpedo battery was essential. Light cruisers employed twin and triple mounts when built. It was not until immediately before the war that a select few of the 5,500-ton cruisers received the new Type 92 quadruple torpedo mounts. Even so, the broadside of 15 of the light cruisers was an underwhelming four weapons compared to the eight or nine torpedo broadside of the newest Japanese destroyers. Only a handful of the light cruisers were equipped with the Type 93

**Key**

1. 5.5-inch (14cm) Type 3 gun (6 – 5 shown)
2. Kure Type No. 2 Catapult Model 3
3. Aircraft crane
4. Mainmast
5. Type 92 43-inch (110cm) searchlight (3)
6. Type 96 25mm triple mount (2)
7. Type 90 radio direction finder antenna
8. Secondary rangefinder
9. Type 96 25mm twin mount (2 – 1 shown)
10. 30-ft (9 meter) cutter (3 shown)
11. Foremast
12. No. 21 air and surface search radar
13. Fire command platform
14. Target survey platform
15. 13-ft (4 meter) Rangefinder
16. 5-ft (1.5 meter) navigational rangefinder tower (2 – one not shown)
17. Navigational bridge
18. 13mm quad mount
19. Boiler room 1
20. Type 8 24-inch (61cm) twin torpedo mount (4 total – 2 shown)
21. Boiler room 2
22. 36-ft (11 meter) motor boat
23. Boiler room 3
24. Boiler room 4
25. Forward engine room
26. Aft engine room

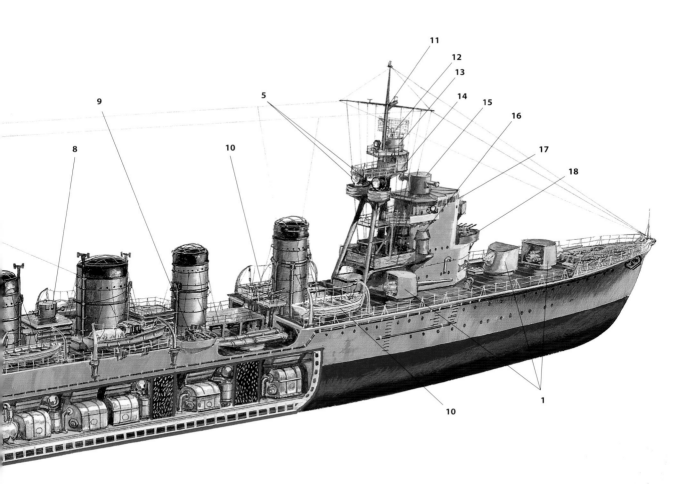

Model 1, Modification 2 torpedo before the start of the war. This remarkable weapon, later given the nickname "Long Lance" by the Allies, possessed a 1,082-pound warhead and was high-speed and wakeless. It could travel up to 43,746 yards at 36 knots, or 35,000 yards at 40 knots, or 21,873 yards at 48 knots. The majority of light cruisers went to war with the 24-inch Type 90 torpedo introduced in 1931. This weapon had a maximum range of 16,350 yards at 35 knots and a warhead of 827 pounds.

*Tama* shown in January 1942 after receiving its camouflage in December 1941. *Tama* spent much of its wartime career in northern waters and acted at various times as flagship of *Sentai* 21 and the Fifth Fleet. (Yamato Museum)

## Heavy Antiaircraft Armament

Japanese light cruisers began the Pacific War with no long-range antiaircraft weapon. Most of the 5,500-ton cruisers eventually received a single Type 89 5-inch (127mm) twin mount. This was the standard Japanese long-range antiaircraft weapon of the war. The Type 89 gun was a decent design but suffered from a relatively short maximum range. On the light cruisers, the Type 89 was further handicapped by the absence of a dedicated fire-control system. A new 3.15-inch (30mm) gun was developed for the Agano class, but each ship received only two of the twin mounts. The best Japanese Navy long-range antiaircraft gun of the war was the Type 98 3.9-inch (100mm) twin gun, which was fitted on the *Oyodo*, as well as the Akizuki class of antiaircraft destroyers and the carrier *Taiho*. It possessed a high muzzle velocity, superb range, and was considered an excellent gun by the Japanese.

| Japanese Light Cruiser Heavy Antiaircraft Guns | | | | |
|---|---|---|---|---|
| Type | Class | Max. Elevation (degrees) | Max. Effective Vertical Range (yards) | Rate of Fire (rounds/minute) |
| Type 3 3.15 inch/40 caliber | All pre-war | 75 | 5,775 | 13 |
| Type 10 4.7 inch/45 caliber | Yubari | 75 | 9,240 | 6–8 |
| Type 89 5 inch/40 caliber | Kuma, Nagara, Sendai, Katori | 90 | 8,090 | 11–12 |
| Type 98 3.15 inch/60 caliber | Agano | 90 | 9,920 | 25 |
| Type 98 3.9 inch/65 caliber | Oyodo | 90 | 11,9 | 15 |

## Light Antiaircraft Armament

Going into the war, Japanese light cruisers possessed an inadequate light antiaircraft fit. Standard fit at the beginning of the war was a paltry two Type 96 twin 25mm mounts positioned near the forward stack and a quad 13mm machine gun in front of the bridge. No antiaircraft weapon heavier than the 25mm gun was provided. The Type 96 was destined to become the standard light antiaircraft weapon of the Imperial Navy and was produced in single (1943), and double and triple (1941) mounts. The original twin gun version was developed by the French firm Hotchkiss and adopted by the Imperial Navy in 1936. Though the Japanese were inexplicably happy with this weapon, even they saw it had many shortcomings. These included low training and elevating speeds, excessive muzzle blast, and a rate of fire that was reduced by the need to keep reloading 15-round magazines. The single 25mm gun proved difficult for individual crewmen to handle. To increase the vulnerability of the light cruisers to air attack, the 25mm were usually not provided with a dedicated fire-control system so the gunners were forced to rely on visual tracking. Despite the growing profusion of 25mm guns on light cruisers during the war, these ships grew increasingly vulnerable to air attack.

**OPPOSITE**
This view of *Sakawa* after the war in Sasebo shows the bridge structure of an Agano-class cruiser. The No. 21 air search radar can be seen on the front of the rangefinder tower and the No. 13 radar can be seen on the trailing edge of the foremast. The double-horn shape of the No. 22 surface search radar is evident at the base of the rangefinder tower. (Author's collection)

**Japanese Light Cruiser Names**

Per instructions dating from 1912, cruisers with a displacement of less than 7,000 tons were classified as second-class cruisers. Both the American and British navies had begun calling their smaller cruisers "light cruisers"; unofficially, the Japanese followed suit. In 1930, the London Naval Treaty codified the division of ships into "heavy" and "light" cruiser designations. In 1913 the Navy Minister issued instructions that second-class cruisers were to be named after rivers or streams. First-class, later heavy, cruisers, were named after mountains. However, this distinction became confused because of the fact that six ships designed and built in the aftermath of the London Treaty as light cruisers retained their original river and stream names after they were converted to heavy cruisers before the war. The three training ships of the Katori class were not actually considered cruisers, so were not named after streams. Rather, they were named after famous shrines of Japan.

*Tenryu* – a river flowing through three prefectures in central Honshu
*Tatsuta* – a stream in Nara Prefecture in central Honshu
*Kuma* – a river flowing through Kumamoto Prefecture in eastern Kyushu
*Tama* – a river in southeastern Tokyo
*Kitakami* – a river flowing through northeastern Honshu
*Isuzu* – a river in Mie Prefecture in southern Honshu
*Natori* – a river in Miyagi Prefecture in northeastern Honshu
*Nagara* – a river flowing through Mie Prefecture in southern Honshu
*Yura* – a river in Kyoto Prefecture in central Honshu
*Abukuma* – a river flowing through two prefectures in northeastern Honshu
*Kinu* – a river flowing through two prefectures north of Tokyo
*Sendai* – a river that originates and flows through Kagoshima Prefecture in the southwestern tip of Kyushu
*Jintsu* – a river flowing through Toyama Prefecture, emptying into the Sea of Japan
*Naka* – a river flowing through two prefectures north of Tokyo
*Yubari* – a river on Hokkaido that begins in Mount Yubari
*Agano* – a stream in Niigata Prefecture in northern Honshu
*Noshiro* – a stream in Akita Prefecture in northern Honshu
*Yahagi* – a stream in Aichi Prefecture in central Honshu
*Sakawa* – a stream in Kanagawa Prefecture near Mount Fuji
*Oyodo* – a stream in Miyazaki Prefecture on Kyushu
*Katori* – a Shinto shrine in Chiba Prefecture
*Kashima* – a Shinto Shrine in Iraraki Prefecture
*Kashii* – a Shinto Shrine in Fukuoka Prefecture

| Type 96 25mm Gun (1936) | |
| --- | --- |
| Muzzle Velocity | 984 yards/second |
| Rate of Fire | |
| Theoretical | 220–240 rounds/minute |
| Actual | 110–120 rounds/minute |
| Antiaircraft Range | |
| Maximum | 8,200 yards |
| Effective | 766–1,633 yards |
| Shell Weight | 8.8 ounces |

## Radar

The Japanese began to equip their light cruisers with radar in mid-1943. This modification occurred when the ships returned to Japan for repair and refit. The most common light cruiser radar was an air-search radar known formally as the Type 2 (1942) shipboard search radar Model 1 Modification 2, or abbreviated as No. 21 (2). The No. 21 (2) radar had a mattress antenna. On light cruisers, it was fitted in several places, including on top of the bridge structure, on top of the fire-control station on the foremast, and, on the modern light cruisers, on the face of the rangefinder on top of the rangefinder tower. A few light cruisers also received another air search radar, which was introduced later in 1943 and designated as the No. 13 (Type 3, No.1, Model 3). This had a long ladder antenna and was usually fitted on the mainmast of light cruisers. The final type of cruiser radar was the No. 22 Modification 4M radar, designed for surface search. This had a twin-horn antenna design, one for transmitting and one for receiving. It was usually mounted in pairs on both sides of the bridge or on the foremast.

For surface targets, the No. 22 (4) could detect a battleship target at 38,276 yards, a cruiser-sized ship at 21,872 yards, and a destroyer-sized target at 18,591 yards. The range error was 820–1,640 feet and the bearing error up to three degrees.

| Japanese Light Cruiser Radars | | | |
|---|---|---|---|
| | No. 21 Mod. 2 | No. 13 | No. 22 Mod. 4M |
| Peak Power Output | 5 kW | 10 kW | 2 kW |
| Maximum Range | 93 miles | 93 miles | 37 miles |
| Effective Range | | | |
| Single aircraft | 43 miles | 31 miles | 11 miles |
| Group of aircraft | 62 miles | 62 miles | 22 miles |
| Accuracy | 1,094–2,187 yards | 2,187–3,280 yards | 273–546 yards |
| Bearing Accuracy | 5–8 degrees | 10 degrees | 3 degrees |

# THE LIGHT CRUISER CLASSES

## Tenryu Class
### Design and Construction
In May 1916, the Imperial Navy began construction of its first class of modern cruisers. The two ships, loosely based on the British C- and D- class light cruisers, were named *Tenryu* and *Tatsuta* and were designed as destroyer squadron leaders. However, at only 3,500 tons, they were soon rendered too small and too slow by the latest Japanese destroyer designs. Newer Japanese destroyers of the period, like the Minekaze class, had a design speed of 39 knots, compared to the Tenryu's 33 knots. The new cruisers were also deficient in firepower, especially when compared to the new class of American scout cruisers of the Omaha class.

High speed was an important design consideration. Several weight-saving measures were used and a high length-to-beam ratio adopted. Three sets of destroyer turbines were fitted and ten boilers installed in three boiler rooms. Two of these were mixed-firing boilers using oil and coal.

Protection of the hull was designed to defeat 4-inch shell fire from American destroyers. Total armor was only 4.2 percent of displacement. Interior armor in the main belt of 25mm was supplemented by outer armor of between 25 and 38mm. Deck armor was 22–35mm thick. The class featured a simple and small bridge with conning tower armor of 51mm.

| Tenryu Class Construction | | | | |
|---|---|---|---|---|
| Ship | Built at | Laid down | Launched | Completed |
| *Tenryu* | Yokosuka NY | 5/17/17 | 3/11/18 | 11/20/19 |
| *Tatsuta* | Sasebo NY | 7/24/17 | 5/29/18 | 3/31/19 |

## Armament

As completed, the main armament was four Type 3 5.5-inch guns. All were single mounts and all were situated on the centerline. Fire control for the main battery was provided by a fire-control director located in the foremast. Rangefinding was provided by two 8-foot-long rangefinders, one on the bridge and one on the aft superstructure. Antiaircraft armament was a single Type 3 3.15-inch high-angle gun mounted aft, and two 6.5mm machine guns amidships. The torpedo armament was two triple centerline Type 6 21-inch triple mounts. These were the first triple mounts fitted in any ship in the Imperial Navy. There were no reloads.

## Service Modifications

Between completion and 1940, neither ship received significant modifications. Consideration was given to converting both ships into antiaircraft cruisers in 1935–36, with each ship mounting four Type 89 twin 5-inch high-angle guns, but lack of space in shipyards made this impossible. In 1938–39, more thought was given to conversion into an antiaircraft cruiser, with the new Type 98 3.15-inch twin mounts, but this was also dropped. In November 1940, in preparation for war, both ships were lightly modernized. The 3.15-inch antiaircraft gun was removed, as were the 13mm machine guns fitted in 1937, replaced by two Type 96 twin 25mm guns placed abreast the forward stack. The compass bridge received a permanent cover and the mixed-firing boilers were converted to oil only.

Since both units were considered second-line units by 1939, wartime modifications were minor. Between February 23 and 27, 1942, while at Truk, both cruisers received two twin 25mm mounts aft. No other modifications were made to *Tenryu* before it was lost, but *Tatsuta* received a fifth 25mm twin mount and possibly a No. 21 or 22 radar during an August–September 1943 refit.

## Wartime Service

The two ships of the Tenryu class began the war comprising *Sentai* (Squadron) 18. Their first combat operation was the seizure of Wake Island. The first attempt on December 11 failed, but the second attempt on December 23 succeeded. Though the Japanese suffered heavy losses in the operation, neither cruiser was damaged. Next, *Sentai* 18 participated in the invasion of Rabaul and Kavieng in January.

On March 8, the cruisers provided cover for the seizure of Lae and Salamaua on the northeastern coast of New Guinea. In response, the Americans attacked the invasion force on March 10 with carrier aircraft, but neither ship was damaged. Subsequently, both ships covered landings at Bougainville, Shortland, and Manus Island through April 8.

The next major operation for *Sentai* 18 was the invasion of Port Moresby and Tulagi. As part of the Cover Force for the operation, they were charged with establishing seaplane bases to support the invasion. Though Tulagi was captured on May 3, the Japanese were thwarted in their attempt to land at Port Moresby, their first strategic defeat of the war. Both ships returned to Japan in late May for a brief overhaul, and were back at Truk on June 23.

*Sentai* 18 escorted construction troops to Guadalcanal on July 6. On August 7, American forces landed on Guadalcanal to seize the airfield there. *Tenryu* was part of the Japanese force scraped together to attack the American beachhead. It acquitted itself well. Two of its torpedoes were credited with hitting heavy cruiser *Quincy*, which later sank. It engaged two American destroyers at different times in the battle, and hit one. In return, it took a single

This exceptionally clear 1933 view shows a port side view of *Tenryu*. The ship's austere design is evident with its small bridge structure and weak four 5.5-inch gun main armament. (Yamato Museum)

5-inch round from cruiser *Chicago*, which wounded two. In total, *Tenryu* fired 80 5.5-inch shells and all six of its torpedoes.

Both ships were active in constant convoy duty from Rabaul to various points on New Guinea and Guadalcanal throughout 1942. This included the landing of a Japanese invasion force at Milne Bay on August 25 and their evacuation on September 5–6. *Tatsuta* landed the commander of the 17th Army on Guadalcanal on October 9. *Tenryu* was hit by a bomb from a B-17 while anchored in Rabaul on October 2. Twenty-three men were killed, but the ship was repaired locally.

In December, *Tenryu* was designated as the flagship of the Madang Attack Force to move troops to Madang on northeastern New Guinea. On December 18, after leaving Madang, *Tenryu* was hit by two torpedoes from American submarine *Albacore* and sunk. Casualties included 23 dead and 21 wounded.

*Tatsuta* departed for Japan to repair rudder damage in January 1943. After completion, it was retained in home waters as flagship of Destroyer Squadron 11, which was comprised of new destroyers conducting shakedown cruises. *Tatsuta* remained on training duties into 1944 with the exception of one run to Truk in October 1943. In February 1944 *Tatsuta* prepared for an emergency transport mission to the Central Pacific. While bound for Saipan, it was hit by two torpedoes from American submarine *Sand Lance* on March 12 and sunk.

This 1934 view shows a Tenryu-class cruiser at high speed with its torpedo tubes trained to starboard. The two aft 5.5-inch guns are discernable in this blurry image. The dark color of the linoleum deck covering compared to the standard gray color of the rest of the ship can also be seen. (*Ships of the World* magazine)

| Tenryu Class Specifications | |
| --- | --- |
| Displacement | 3,230 tons standard*; 4,621 tons full load (1919) |
| Dimensions | Length: 468ft overall / Beam 40.5ft / Draft 24.5ft |
| Speed | 33 knots |
| Range | 5,000nm at 14 knots |
| Crew | 33 officers and 304 enlisted personnel plus space for staff |

\* Standard displacement was adopted by the Japanese in 1921 in response to the Washington Naval Treaty. It was the weight of the ship with a full load of stores and ammunition, but with no fuel, lubricating oil and reserve feed water.

## Kuma Class
### Design and Construction

The first two 5,500-ton cruisers, named *Kuma* and *Tama*, were ordered in 1917, and the class became known after the lead ship *Kuma*. As the first of the 5,500-ton units, the class was also known as the 5,500-Ton Model I. The next three 5,500-Ton Model I ships were ordered in 1918.

Plans for the Kuma class were being drawn up as the Tenryu class was under construction. The move from a 3,500-ton ship up to a 5,500-ton design allowed many improvements to be incorporated. To address one of the weaknesses of the Tenryu class, the Kuma class had a longer hull and more powerful machinery in order to attain its design speed of 36 knots necessary to operate with the newer destroyers. A higher freeboard made the ships more seaworthy and provided more crew living space. The ships of the Kuma class were considered to be good sea boats.

Like the Tenryu class, the Kuma-class ships had a light bridge structure, abaft of which was a tripod mast on which the fire-control platform was located, along with two searchlights. There was also a small aft superstructure abaft the pole mainmast.

The last unit of the Kuma class, *Kiso*, was built with a 30-foot flying-off platform forward-mounted above the first two turrets. The platform was removed in 1922, but the superstructure retained the shape of the hangar.

Protection was still limited to that required to defeat a 4-inch shell. The side belt featured an internal 25mm of armor and an 38mm external plate; the armored deck was 29mm thick.

The design speed was 36 knots, which required 90,000 shaft horsepower (SHP). Four shafts were used, each driven by a 22,500 SHP turbine. Twelve boilers were fitted, including a small number of mixed-firing boilers (two in the Kuma and Nagara class, and four in the Sendai class).

**Kuma Class Construction**

| Ship | Built at | Laid down | Launched | Completed |
| --- | --- | --- | --- | --- |
| *Kuma* | Sasebo NY | 8/29/18 | 7/14/19 | 8/31/20 |
| *Tama* | Nagasaki, by Mitsubishi | 8/10/18 | 2/10/20 | 1/29/21 |
| *Kiso* | Nagasaki, by Mitsubishi | 6/10/19 | 7/15/20 | 5/4/21 |
| *Oi* | Kobe, by Kawasaki | 11/24/19 | 7/15/20 | 10/3/21 |
| *Kitakami* | Sasebo NY | 9/1/19 | 7/3/20 | 4/15/21 |

## Armament

The main battery on the first 5,500-ton cruiser class was increased to seven single 5.5-inch guns. Two were placed forward, two on each side of the forward superstructure, and three aft, which meant that only six guns could fire broadside. This was the standard layout maintained for the next two classes of 5,500-ton cruisers. Fire control was provided by a director mounted on top of the forward tripod mast and by eight-foot rangefinders mounted between the second and third smokestacks. As completed, the antiaircraft armament was limited to two single 3.15-inch guns placed adjacent to the first stack and two 6.5mm machine guns.

The torpedo armament was increased to a total of eight tubes, mounted in four twin mounts. The first set was placed abaft the forward superstructure and the second abaft the third stack. Since they were not placed on the centerline, only four could be fired to each side. Eight reloads were provided.

## Service Modifications

The 14 5,500-ton cruisers were unmodified until the ships underwent a series of modification from 1931 to 1941. The changes were basically the same for all three classes and centered on the ships' aircraft handling arrangements, antiaircraft fit, and alterations to the bridge and superstructure.

The flying platform arrangement forward of the bridge never proved successful in service. After a brief experiment on three ships placed a small catapult in place of the flying platform in 1930-31, it was decided to put a 62-foot catapult on 11 ships (less *Kitakami*, *Oi*, and *Kiso*, which had been demilitarized as required by the London Treaty). On *Kuma* and *Tama* and the six ships of the Nagara class, the catapult was placed aft between the Number 5 and 6 5.5-inch guns. On the three units of the Sendai class, the catapult was placed between the Number 6 and 7 guns. A crane to lift the seaplane from

This fine view from 1935 shows the details of *Kuma*. The light bridge structure is evident, as is the fire-control position on the foremast. Two searchlights are mounted low on the foremast. Three of the four forward 5.5–inch gun mounts are evident as is the twin torpedo mount under the white awning. Just aft of the torpedoes is a single 3.15-inch antiaircraft gun. (Naval History and Heritage Command)

the water was placed on the mainmast, which was converted from a pole to a heavier tripod.

The antiaircraft fit of all 14 ships was improved, and had been largely standardized by 1941 and the start of the war. Compared to foreign light cruisers it remained deficient. The original 3.15-inch single guns were replaced first by twin 13mm mounts and finally by a Type 96 twin 25mm mount. The original 6.5mm machine guns were replaced by 7.7mm mounts. The Nagara and Sendai class units received a quadruple 13mm mount fitted in front of the bridge.

The bridges on the Kuma class were modified in 1932–34. This included covering the compass bridge and building a rangefinder tower above the bridge with either an 11.5-foot or a 13-foot rangefinder. After all modifications, the full-load displacement of the ships exceeded 7,000 tons, which brought maximum speed down to 32–33 knots. To maintain stability, extra ballast was added. *Kiso* had anti-rain caps fitted on two forward smokestacks, which gave it a unique appearance; it retained these until it was sunk.

On August 25, 1941, *Oi* and *Kitakami* were ordered to Sasebo for urgent conversion into "torpedo-cruisers". These ships were to play an important role in the Japanese plan to crush the American battle fleet during a decisive battle. Originally *Oi*, *Kitakami*, and *Kiso* were all to be converted into torpedo cruisers to form a special squadron that had the firepower to deliver a massive torpedo attack. By 1938 it was clear that there were insufficient Type 92 quadruple mounts, so *Kiso* was not modified. The actual conversion was not carried out until definite war preparations were begun so that the Americans would not gain knowledge of the creation of the torpedo cruisers. The conversion was to be very extensive, with all existing armament removed and replaced by four twin Type 89 high-angle mounts, four twin Type 96 twin 25mm mounts, and 11 quadruple torpedo mounts. When the ships arrived in the yards in August 1941, there were insufficient Type 89 mounts and torpedo tubes. The conversion was modified to retain the four forward 5.5-inch guns and remove the aft three. Only ten quadruple torpedo mounts were fitted per ship; five on each side with a total of 40 torpedoes. No reloads were carried, but provisions were made to transfer torpedoes between mounts if necessary. Two twin 25mm guns were placed abreast of the first stack. The torpedo fire-control station in the foremast was modified to allow torpedo combat at ranges greater than 32,700 yards. Both ships received a 20-foot rangefinder above the compass bridge. The displacement increased to 5,860 tons standard displacement and speed dropped to 31.67 knots in a December 1941 speed trial on *Kitakami*.

Kuma-class wartime modifications centered around augmenting the antiaircraft armament. To do this, most ships had at least one of their 5.5-inch

**B**    **THE KUMA CLASS**

This plate shows three ships of the Kuma class at different points of the war. *Tama* is shown in the top profile in its 1942 configuration. Note the camouflage scheme unique to her, the placement of the 5.5-inch guns, and the catapult aft. The middle profile is *Kiso* in its late war 1944 configuration. The primary difference with the earlier view of *Tama* is the removal of two of the aft 5.5-inch guns and the profusion of 25mm and 13mm guns for antiaircraft defense. Also note the radar on top of the foremast. *Kiso* was not fitted with a catapult before the war; also note the rain catchers on the two forward stacks. The bottom profile is *Kitakami* in its torpedo cruiser configuration. While the forward part of the ship remained basically unaltered, the placement of the five starboard side Type 92 quadruple torpedo launchers can be readily seen as well as the modified stern portion of the ship.

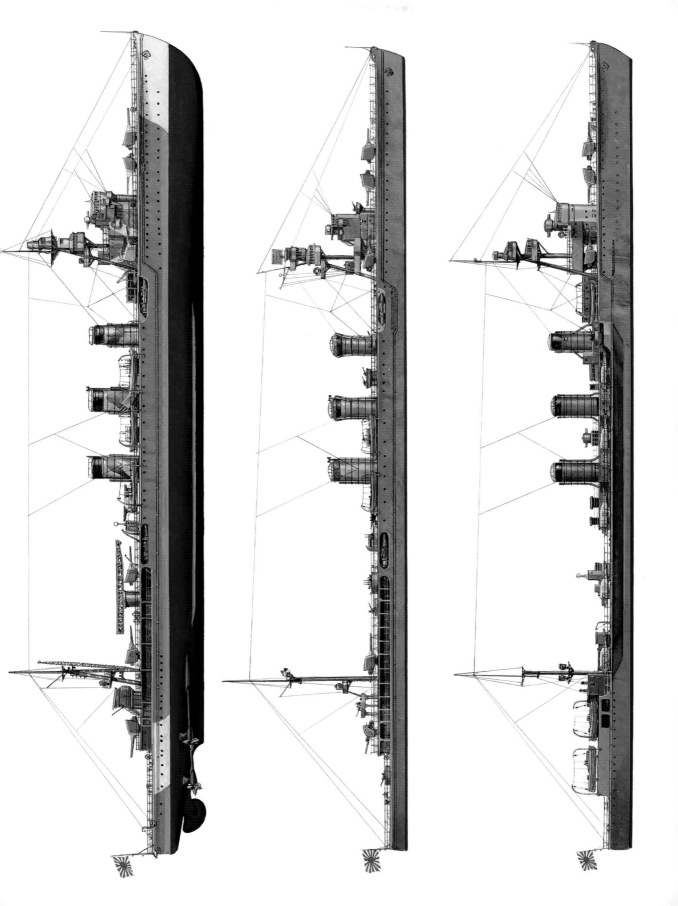

In the same sequence of photographs taken at Tsingtao, China, on July 16, 1935 comes this fine view of *Kuma*'s aft section. The three aft 5.5-inch guns are clearly shown and the aft twin torpedo tube mount has been swung out. The catapult between gun mounts No. 5 and 6 carried a single reconnaissance seaplane, in this case the Type 90-3; this aircraft was obsolete by the start of the war and was replaced by the Kawanishi E7K2 Type 94. (Naval History and Heritage Command)

single guns and their catapult removed. In 1943 a couple of twin or triple 25mm mounts were added. Later in 1943 and into 1944, *Tama* and *Kiso* received a Type 89 twin 5-inch gun in addition to as many as 18 single 25mm guns and additional triple mounts. *Kuma* never carried radar, but *Tama* and *Kiso* received a No. 21 set on top of the foremast and a No. 22 farther down.

*Oi* and *Kitakami* went through several major changes after their conversion into torpedo cruisers. The first occurred in August 1942 when they were modified as fast transports in order to operate in the Solomons area. This entailed the removal of the four aft quadruple torpedo mounts, which were replaced with two 46-foot barges. In addition, two triple 25mm mounts were fitted aft, and depth charge rails provided. A more drastic fast transport conversion was planned in May 1943, but never carried out.

After *Kitakami* was torpedoed in January 1944, it was decided to convert it into a *kaiten* carrier. The *kaiten* was a piloted version of the Type 93 long-range torpedo. Since it had the benefit of human guidance and was expected to be very accurate, it was seen as a potentially devastating weapon. Work began in August and was based on the unfulfilled plans for a complete conversion into fast transports. The work was extensive and not finished until November. All armament was stripped and replaced with two Type 89 mounts (one forward, one aft) and a total of 67 25mm guns (12 triple and 31 single mounts). Two depth charge rails and two throwers were also fitted. The ship's main armament now became eight Model 1 *kaitens*, which were carried and launched on two sets of rails mounted aft on each side of the ship. One could be launched every eight minutes. The removal of the aft turbines reduced the ship's top speed to 23 knots. The bridge was modified, and the torpedo direction equipment removed and replaced by additional antiaircraft fire-control equipment. Two No. 13 air-search radars and a No. 22 set were fitted. Crew size rose to 615.

| Kuma Class Modifications (final configuration when lost) | | | | | |
|---|---|---|---|---|---|
| Ship | Kuma | Tama | Kiso | Oi | Kitakami |
| Torpedo tubes | 8 (2x4) | 8 (2x4) | 8 (2x4) | 24 (4x6) | 0 |
| 5.5-inch guns | 6 | 5 | 5 | 4 | 0 |
| Type 89 twin 5-inch guns | 0 | 1 | 1 | 0 | 2 |
| Triple 25mm guns | 2 | 5 | 4 | 2 | 12 |
| Twin 25mm guns | 2 | 4 | 4 | 2 | 0 |
| Single 25mm guns | 0 | 18 | 18 | 0 | 31 |
| 13mm guns | 0 | 7 | 10 | 0 | 0 |
| Radar | None | No. 21, 22 | No. 21, 22 | None | No. 13 (2), 22 |

### Wartime Service

*Kuma* participated in the invasion of the Philippines and then remained there as part of the local defense forces. Subsequently it became part of the Southwest Area Fleet, responsible for defending the Dutch East Indies. *Kuma* underwent a refit in October–November 1943 at Singapore. On January 11, while operating out of Penang, it was hit by two torpedoes fired from the British submarine

*Tally Ho.* It quickly sank by the stern with a loss of 138 men.

*Tama* and *Kiso* began the war assigned to *Sentai* 21 and spent much of their careers serving together. *Sentai* 21 was assigned to the Fifth Fleet and was responsible for defending the North Pacific. Both cruisers were camouflaged with white bows and sterns, and white patches

on their superstructure to blend in with the northern Pacific environment. Both were assigned to the Kiska Seizure Force in June 1942. During this operation, Kiska was taken on June 7, 1942 followed by Attu Island. These two islands became the focal points of the Aleutians campaign.

In March, the Imperial Navy attempted to run a convoy to Attu Island. This resulted in the battle of Komandorski Islands on March 27, 1943 when the Americans decided to contest the Japanese plan. *Tama* was part of the Japanese force assigned to escort the convoy, and which failed to reach its destination in the face of a smaller American force. During the battle, *Tama* fired 136 5.5-inch shells and four torpedoes, receiving only two 5-inch hits in return, both on the catapult, which wounded only one.

After the Americans regained Attu in May 1943, *Tama* and *Kiso* took part in the successful evacuation of the garrison from Kiska on July 29. *Kiso* took 1,189 Japanese Army personnel to safety. Next, the cruisers were shifted to the South Pacific to act as fast transports. In October 1943 near Rabaul, *Tama* incurred a near miss from an aircraft bomb and *Kiso* took a direct hit. *Tama* and *Kiso* returned to Japan in late 1943 for major modification. Following completion, they resumed transport duties to the Bonin Islands and homeland defense duties. Both units were committed to the Imperial Navy's all-out effort to repel the American invasion of the Philippines in October 1944. *Tama* was assigned to the Mobile (Carrier) Force. On October 25, this force came under attack from American carrier aircraft. *Tama* was hit by an aircraft torpedo and eventually limped unescorted to Okinawa at 14 knots. It was detected and attacked by American submarine *Jallao*, which hit it with three torpedoes. *Tama* sank quickly with the loss of all hands.

*Kiso* was assigned duties to reinforce the Philippines. It departed Japan on October 27 and arrived in Manila on November 10. On November 13, while under way in Manila Bay, it was attacked by American carrier aircraft and hit by three bombs. These resulted in a heavy loss of life (only 104 of 819 crewmen were saved) and the ship gradually sank. The wreck remained eight miles off Manila until it was refloated for scrapping in 1955.

*Oi* and *Kitakami* began the war assigned to *Sentai* 9. Both remained in home waters until the Midway operation where they were part of the Main Body and saw no action. In August 1942, both were converted into high-speed transports, which led them to transport missions out of Truk and Rabaul until March 1943. From March 1943, both were assigned to the Southwest Area Fleet where they conducted escort and transport duties. While serving in this capacity, *Oi* was hit by two torpedoes from the American submarine

This prewar view of *Kiso* shows its unique bridge structure. Of the Kuma-class cruisers, only *Kiso* received the aircraft hangar in the front of the bridge, which made its bridge higher than other ships in the class. *Kiso* also has flared stacks on its first two stacks, another unique feature. (Naval History and Heritage Command)

*Kitakami* in January 1945 after its conversion into a *kaiten* carrier. The ship was provided with an entirely new antiaircraft suite and fire-control system. A No. 22 radar is visible on the second platform of the foremast and a No. 13 radar is mounted on top of the foremast. A second No. 13 set was placed on the mainmast aft. The *kaitens* were carried on rails where the torpedo tubes were previously located and were launched over the rounded stern. (Yamato Museum)

*Flasher* on July 19, 1944, after leaving Manila. The resulting flooding could not be checked and the ship sank that afternoon with the loss of 153 men.

*Kitakami* also fell victim to submarine torpedoes, in this case to two weapons from the British submarine *Templar* on January 27, 1944. However, the ship survived and returned to Singapore for repairs. After returning to Japan in August 1944, it began a conversion into a *kaiten* carrier. In this capacity, it saw little service due to a lack of fuel. On July 24, 1945 it was attacked by carrier aircraft in the Kure area. *Kitakami* suffered ten near misses from bombs, and these sufficed to disable its engines, rendering it immobile. After the war it was towed to Kagoshima where it was used as a repair ship for units involved in repatriation services. The cruiser was finally scrapped in 1946–47.

| Kuma Class Specifications | |
|---|---|
| Displacement | 5,100 tons standard; 5,500 tons normal* 7,094 tons full load (1920) |
| Dimensions | Length: 532ft overall / Beam: 46.5ft / Draft: 29ft |
| Speed | 36 knots |
| Range | 6,000nm at 14 knots (actual) |
| Crew | 37 officers and 413 enlisted personnel plus space for staff (5 officers and 22 enlisted) |

\* Normal displacement differed from standard displacement by adding ¼ fuel oil, ½ lubricating oil, but adding lesser amounts of ammunition and other stores.

## Nagara Class
### Design and Construction
The final three 5,500-ton units authorized in the 8-4 Fleet Completion Program were ordered in the fiscal year 1920. Since these ships were different from the Kuma class, they were known as the modified Kuma class, or more commonly as the Nagara class, after the lead unit in the class. They were also referred to as 5,500-Ton Model II. The second set of three Nagara-class ships were laid down later in 1920.

The Nagara class was similar to the Kuma class, using the same hull shape, the same power plant, and the same layout for the main armament. The principal difference was the construction of the bridge, which was modified to accommodate an aircraft hangar. The Nagara class employed a very short flying-off platform for aircraft, and a hangar placed in the front of the forward superstructure below the bridge. In turn, this made the bridge level higher. A 33-foot platform was fitted above the Number 2 gun. There was no provision made for returning the seaplane to the ship. This arrangement proved impractical and was quickly replaced with a catapult in place of the platform.

Another difference was the incorporation of the new 24-inch torpedoes, which required larger torpedo tubes. Also, the main deck was extended aft so that it covered the aft set of torpedo tubes. There was no aft superstructure.

| Nagara Class Construction | | | | |
|---|---|---|---|---|
| Ship | Built at | Laid down | Launched | Completed |
| *Nagara* | Sasebo NY | 9/9/20 | 4/25/21 | 4/21/22 |
| *Isuzu* | Nagasaki, by Mitsubishi | 8/10/20 | 10/29/21 | 8/15/23 |
| *Natori* | Nagasaki, by Mitsubishi | 12/14/20 | 2/16/22 | 9/15/22 |
| *Yura* | Sasebo NY | 5/21/21 | 2/15/22 | 3/20/23 |
| *Kinu* | Kobe, by Kawasaki | 1/17/21 | 5/29/22 | 11/10/22 |
| *Abukuma* | Nagasaki, by Mitsubishi | 12/8/21 | 3/16/23 | 5/26/25 |

*Kiso* in its northern waters' camouflage scheme, which it wore from December 1941. The ship is identifiable by its unique camouflage and its two forward flared stacks. The positions of the white canvas-covered torpedo mounts can also be seen. (*Ships of the World* magazine)

## Armament

As originally built, the armament of the Nagara class was identical to that of the Kuma class. The only exception was the provision of 24-inch torpedoes, replacing the 21-inch weapons of the previous class.

## Service Modifications

The aircraft-handling arrangement located in front of the bridge proved a failure. This led to a bridge-modification program, which was carried out 1929–34. Each ship emerged with a different bridge arrangement, but all had their catapult moved aft to a position between 5.5-inch guns Number 5 and 6. The superstructure had a rangefinder tower built on top of the bridge, equipped with a main rangefinder. This was a 20-foot instrument on *Abukuma*, 15-foot on *Nagara* and *Isuzu*, 13-foot on Natori, and 12-foot on *Yura* and *Kinu*. By the start of the war, the 3.15-inch antiaircraft guns had been replaced with two twin 25mm mounts.

As war neared, *Abukuma* and *Kinu*, as flagships of destroyer squadrons, were earmarked to receive the new Type 93 torpedoes. However, shortages meant that only *Abukuma* received quadruple mounts in place of the aft twin mounts between March and May 1941. Sixteen Type 93 torpedoes were embarked, including eight reloads. The forward twin torpedo mounts were also removed.

Wartime modifications were similar to those made to the Kuma class. As shown in the chart below, all but one of the Nagara class (except *Yura*) underwent several changes and no two units were modified in the exact same way. As with the Kuma class, the focus of wartime modification work was the improvement of the ships' weak antiaircraft armament. To keep topweight within acceptable limits and to provide arcs of fire for the new weapons, this required that some of the existing 5.5-inch guns and the ships' catapults be removed. On almost all ships, the guns removed were the Number 5 and 7 mounts aft. In the place of the Number 7 mount, a Type 89 twin 5-inch high-angle mount was fitted. Light antiaircraft guns were added in two phases. In the first phase, usually in 1943 into early 1944, additional 25mm twin or triple mounts were added in the area of the aft torpedo tubes abaft the third stack. In the second phase, the Japanese added 25mm mounts wherever there was an adequate firing arc. This included triple 25mm mounts aft and a number of single 25mm guns, up to 24, throughout the ship. The light antiaircraft fit was further augmented by a number of 13mm guns, usually positioned on the bridge (replacing the 13mm quadruple mount in front of the bridge) and on elevated positions between the stacks.

On some ships (*Nagara* and *Isuzu*) the twin torpedo tubes were replaced with quadruple mounts. These replaced the aft mounts and included the removal of the forward mounts. Most ships also received depth charge racks fitted on the stern.

This is the wreck of *Kiso* pictured on March 15, 1945 off the Manila waterfront. The ship was sunk by air attack on November 13, 1944 and not raised until after the war. The gun aft is the Type 89 twin 5-inch mount added in 1944. The tops of *Kiso's* first two stacks were flared providing a recognition feature for the ship. (Naval History and Heritage Command)

Radar was also fitted to five of the ships. This was most often the No. 21 air-search radar. Two ships, *Isuzu* and *Nagara*, had the No. 21 set placed on top of the bridge structure. *Abukuma*, *Natori*, and *Kinu* had the same radar placed on top of the fire-control station on the foremast. The first ship to receive radar was *Abukuma* in April–May 1943 and the last was *Natori* in 1944.

*Isuzu* was the only Japanese light cruiser that underwent a conversion into an antiaircraft cruiser. Work began in May 1944 and lasted until September. All of the single 5.5-inch mounts were removed and replaced by two additional Type 89 twin mounts for a total of three. A Type 94 high-angle fire-control system was fitted on the foremast. The light antiaircraft armament was increased to 50 (11 triple and 17 single). All four twin torpedo mounts were removed and replaced with two quadruple mounts aft. The catapult was also removed. A complete radar suite was added; the No. 21 radar remained above the bridge, and a No. 13 and a No. 22 were added to the mainmast. For antisubmarine duties, a hydrophone and sonar were fitted, and two depth charge rails added on the stern.

| Nagara Class Modifications (final configuration when lost) | | | | | | |
|---|---|---|---|---|---|---|
| Ship | Nagara | Isuzu | Natori | Yura | Kinu | Abukuma |
| Torpedo tubes | 8 (2x4) | 8 (2x4) | 8 (4x2) | 8 (4x2) | 8 (4x2) | 8 (2x4) |
| 5.5-inch guns | 5 | 0 | 5 | 7 | 5 | 5 |
| Type 89 twin 5-inch guns | 1 | 3 | 1 | 0 | 1 | 1 |
| Triple 25mm guns | 2 | 11 | 2 | 0 | 2 | 4 |
| Twin 25mm guns | 6 | 0 | 2 | 2 | 2 | 2 |
| Single 25mm guns | 14 | 17 | 4 | 0 | 0 | 24 |
| 13mm guns | 10 | 0 | 4 | 4 | 4 | 10 |
| Radar | No. 21 | Nos. 13, 21, 22 | No. 21 | None | No. 21 | Nos. 21, 22 |

## Wartime Service

The six Nagara-class ships enjoyed active and diverse careers. Several acted as flagships for submarine or destroyer squadrons during the war, or were often deployed in transport or local defense missions. Increasingly, as the war went on, they were seen as second-line units and not employed as main fleet forces.

*Nagara* had a long and active career. It began the war assigned to the forces conducting the Philippines invasion and in January and February 1942, participated in the invasion of the Dutch East Indies. In April 1942 *Nagara* was assigned as the flagship of the Destroyer Squadron (Desron) 10. This was the destroyer escort for the First Air Fleet, the Imperial Navy's carrier force. *Nagara's* first operation as a carrier escort was the disastrous Midway operation. *Nagara* remained with the carrier force for the opening phase of the Guadalcanal campaign, participating in the battle of the Eastern Solomons in August. In the second carrier battle of the campaign, the battle of Santa Cruz on October 26, *Nagara* again operated with carrier forces.

*Yura* in December 1923 as completed. The ship is equipped with an aircraft hanger beneath the bridge and a short flying platform. *Yura* was the first 5,500-ton cruiser lost during the war. (Yamato Museum)

In November 1942 *Nagara* and six of its destroyers were committed to the Japanese attempt to reinforce the island. It escorted two battleships ordered to bombard the airfield on November 13. In a savage night battle it sustained one hit on mount No. 7, which killed six and wounded seven. In return, it fired 136 rounds, engaging the American cruisers *San Francisco* and *Atlanta*. *Nagara* returned two nights later in another attempt to bombard the airfield. This time, the Japanese encountered an American force led by two modern battleships. *Nagara* sank the destroyer *Preston* with gunfire, then fired a close-range torpedo broadside at one of the battleships which, unfortunately for the Japanese, all missed.

In November it was assigned as flagship of Destroyer Squadron 4, with the new cruiser *Agano* taking its place as flagship of Desron 10. It supported the evacuation of Guadalcanal in January 1943. In July 1943, Desron 4 was deactivated and *Nagara* became flagship for Desron 2. This lasted until August when it was relieved by the new cruiser *Noshiro*.

In November *Nagara* moved reinforcements to Kwajalein in response to the American invasion of the Marshalls. In this capacity, it was attacked by American carrier aircraft, but suffered only light hull damage from near misses. In May 1944, following a major refit during the war, it was assigned as flagship of Desron 11. In June it began its new career as a fast transport. In this role it was torpedoed by the American submarine *Croaker* on August 7 off Kyushu by a single torpedo. It sank with the loss of 348 men.

*Isuzu* began the war assigned to the forces operating off the Chinese coast. It participated in the seizure of Hong Kong in December 1941 and remained there until April 1942. From there, it operated in the Dutch East Indies into September, when it was designated as the flagship of Desron 2 and was immediately committed to the fierce fighting around Guadalcanal. It screened battleships *Kongo* and *Haruna* when they bombarded Guadalcanal's airfield on October 14. *Isuzu* was again present two nights later when two cruisers conducted another bombardment. It participated in the battle of Santa Cruz on October 26. While covering another cruiser bombardment, it was bombed

*Nagara* in its original configuration from 1926. The ship still carried the hangar in the forward part of the superstructure and the short flying platforms above the first two 5.5-inch mounts. (Yamato Museum)

A starboard quarter view of *Kinu* in January 1937. The location of the catapult between 5.5-inch gun mounts Number 5 and 6 and the addition of the aircraft crane to the mainmast can be seen. The aircraft is a Type 94 reconnaissance seaplane, the standard early war aircraft for the 5,500-ton cruisers equipped with aircraft handling facilities. (Yamato Museum)

on November 14 by U.S. Marine Corps dive-bombers and suffered two near misses, which flooded one of its boiler rooms. It returned to Japan in January for repairs and modification; after its return to service it was assigned transport duties in the Central Pacific. In December 1943 it was attacked by American carrier aircraft at Roi in Kwajalein Atoll. The December 5 attack resulted in three bomb hits aft and several near misses, which killed 20 of its crew. Again, it was forced to return to Japan for repairs. After arriving in Japan, conversion to an antiaircraft cruiser began in May 1944.

After completion, *Isuzu* was assigned to *Sentai* 31, a unit designed to provide antisubmarine protection to fleet units. In this role it took part in the battle of Leyte Gulf as part of the carrier force. This force suffered heavily losing all four of its carriers, but *Isuzu* suffered only light damage when it was attacked by aircraft and came under fire from American surface units while rescuing carrier survivors. In November *Isuzu* made a transport run from Japan to Brunei and was hit in the stern by a single torpedo from the submarine *Hake*. Repairs were made in Surabaja. After completion, it resumed transport duties in the southern area. *Isuzu* became the last 5,500-ton cruiser sunk when on April 7 it was hit by three torpedoes fired from the submarines *Gabilan* and *Charr* in the Dutch East Indies. It sank with the loss of 190 crewmen.

*Natori* also participated in the invasion of the Philippines at the start of the war as the flagship of Desron 5. It later supported the invasion of the Dutch East Indies in January. With its destroyers, *Natori* participated in the battle of Sunda Strait against the American heavy cruiser *Houston* and the Australian cruiser *Perth*. *Natori* fired four torpedoes and 29 rounds at *Perth* and later engaged *Houston*. Both ships were eventually sunk. Subsequently, *Natori* remained in East Indies waters through 1942 into January 1943.

### THE NAGARA CLASS

This plate depicts units of the Nagara class as they appeared throughout the war. The top profile shows *Abukuma* as it appeared during the Pearl Harbor operation. The Nagara class retained the same basic layout as the preceding Kuma class, with some subtle distinctions; the bridge structure was higher and there is no small superstructure aft. The layout of the armament was identical, as was the placement of the catapult. *Abukuma* differed from the other ships in its class as it had its forward twin torpedo tubes removed and the aft set was replaced by a Type 92 quadruple launcher. *Isuzu* is shown in the middle profile after it was converted to an antiaircraft cruiser. It was the most modified Nagara-class ship; all of its 5.5-inch guns have been removed and replaced by three Type 89 twin high-angle 5-inch guns and the number of 25mm gun mounts has been greatly increased. Note the ship carries a full radar suite with a No. 21 set above the bridge, and a No. 13 and No. 22 set on the mainmast aft. *Nagara* is shown in the bottom profile in its late war (1944) configuration. Note that two of its 5.5-inch guns and its catapult have been removed. Additions include a Type 89 5-inch twin mount in place of the Number 7 5.5-inch gun and many 25mm guns. A No. 21 is positioned on top of the bridge.

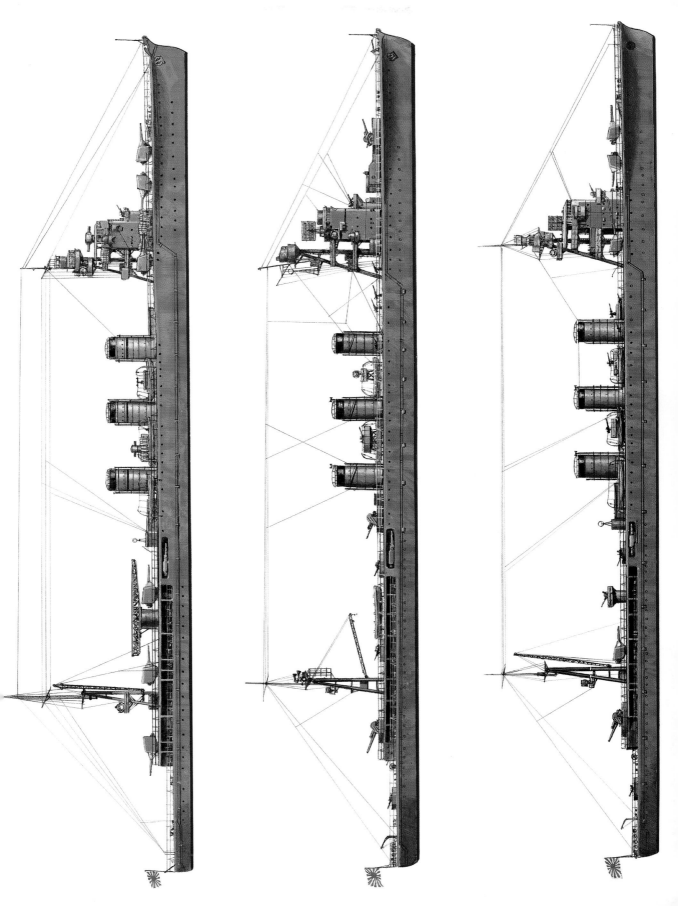

*Natori* shown after its 1933 modification. This view is from 1935 and shows the bridge superstructure after the removal of the hangar and the addition of a platform for the 13mm quadruple mount and a rangefinder tower above the bridge. The foremast includes fire-control facilities for the main gun and torpedo batteries as well as the forward searchlight. The catapult can be seen covered in canvas, abaft the third stack. (Yamato Museum)

*Nagara* departing Kure in 1938. This view shows the box-like shape of the forward superstructure and the platform fitted in front of the bridge for the quad 13mm gun.

On January 9 *Natori* was hit by two torpedoes from the submarine *Tautog*. The stern broke off just aft of No. 7 5.5-inch mount, but the crew was able to control the flooding and reached Singapore for repairs. It arrived in Japan in June 1943 for permanent repairs and modernization, which were not completed until March 1944. *Natori* was then assigned as flagship of Desron 3 and conducted transport missions in the Central Pacific. On August 17, after exiting San Bernardino Strait en route to Palau, it was struck by a single torpedo fired from the submarine *Hardhead*. After a second torpedo struck, the ship sank with the loss of 330 men.

Cruiser *Yura* had the shortest career of the Nagara class. It began the war assigned as flagship of Submarine Squadron 5, which was tasked to support the invasion of Malaya. By late January 1942, *Yura* was assigned to the forces invading the Dutch East Indies. In February it participated in the interception of Allied ships attempting to leave Singapore.

On April 1 *Yura* entered the Indian Ocean in a major Japanese operation to disrupt Allied shipping in the Bay of Bengal. On April 6 it sank three merchant ships. After a brief stop in Japan for an overhaul, *Yura* was assigned as flagship of Desron 4 and in this role participated in the battle of Midway. *Yura* was then committed to the struggle for Guadalcanal, during which it participated in the battle of the Eastern Solomons in August. In September *Yura* moved to Rabaul and suffered slight damage from a B-17 attack while in the Shortland Islands. From here, it escorted supply runs to Guadalcanal. On October 18 *Yura* was hit by a torpedo from submarine *Grampus*, which failed to explode.

One week later *Yura* became the first Japanese light cruiser lost during the war. On October 25 the ship was hit by two bombs from dive-bombers from Henderson Field. The subsequent flooding reduced speed to 14knots and it was decided to beach the vessel. However, before this was done, more dive-bombers and B-17s arrived to place three more bombs on *Yura*. The fires could not be controlled, and the ship was abandoned and scuttled by destroyers.

*Kinu* also began the war assigned as flagship to a submarine squadron, in this case Subron 5, and was first assigned to support the invasion of Malaya. It continued active during the invasion of the Dutch East Indies into March 1942 and on March 1 was slightly damaged by near misses from Australian and New Zealand air attack. After the surrender of the Dutch, it remained in the area until July 1943. On June 23 it was again lightly damaged by air attack, this time from American B-24 bombers.

*Kinu* returned to Japan in August for a refit and modernization. After completion it was again assigned to the southeast area defense forces. In June 1944 the American invasion of Biak Island on the northern coast of New Guinea brought *Kinu* back in the limelight. It was formed into a Transport Force to carry troops from the Philippines to Biak, but the force was spotted by American aircraft and the operation cancelled on June 3. Another attempt involving *Kinu* was cancelled on June 13.

When the Imperial Navy responded to the American invasion of the Philippines in October, *Kinu* was again assigned to a transport force to move units from Mindanao to Leyte. On October 24 the *Kinu* departed Manila and was immediately attacked by carrier aircraft. The ship sustained only light damage from near misses, but 47 of its crew were killed. After delivering the troops (347), *Kinu* was attacked while returning to Manila by aircraft from escort carriers on October 26. A direct hit on the stern and several near misses caused uncontrolled flooding and the ship sank that afternoon.

*Abukuma* began the war as flagship of Desron 1, attached to the Pearl Harbor strike force. *Abukuma* stayed with the carriers as they rampaged through the Pacific up until April, participating in the invasion of Rabaul, the raid on Port Darwin, and the Indian Ocean operation.

After a brief refit, it joined the Fifth Fleet and was assigned to the Adak-Attu Seizure Force. It conducted the invasion of Attu on June 7 and thereafter remained in North Pacific waters, participating in the battle of the Komandorski Islands in March 1943, where it fired 95 5.5-inch rounds and four torpedoes. Undamaged in this indecisive clash, it closed out the Aleutian campaign with the evacuation of Kiska in July, when it carried 1,202 men to safety.

After the evacuation of Kiska, the North Pacific became decidedly a backwater. However, *Abukuma* remained in the Fifth Fleet still as flagship of Desron 1 through July 1944. In October the Fifth Fleet was given a role in the Japanese response to the Leyte invasion. On October 24, *Abukuma* headed for Surigao Strait. Early the next day it was hit by a torpedo launched from an American PT boat and forced to retire. On October 26, while transiting the Sulu Sea, it was attacked by B-24 bombers. Three hits were scored, which started heavy fires. These spread and soon four torpedoes exploded, forcing the crew to abandon ship; 250 died and 283 were rescued.

| Nagara Class Specifications | |
| --- | --- |
| Displacement | 5,170 tons standard; 5,570 tons normal; 7,204 tons full load (1922) |
| Dimensions | Length: 532ft overall / Beam: 46.5ft / Draft: 29ft |
| Speed | 36 knots |
| Range | 6,000nm at 14 knots (actual) |
| Crew | 37 officers and 413 enlisted personnel plus space for staff (5 officers and 22 enlisted) |

## Sendai Class
### Design and Construction
Eight additional 5,500-ton cruisers were planned as part of the 8-8 Fleet Completion Program. The first four were authorized and laid down in 1921. However, the fourth unit was never completed. The final four units, which were scheduled to be built in 1922, were cancelled after the signing of the Washington Treaty when the Japanese decided that future cruiser construction would be focused on heavy cruisers. The three remaining units, *Sendai*, *Jintsu*, and *Naka* were named after the lead unit of the class, and were also known as the modified Nagara class. These ships constituted the 5,500-Ton Model III type.

The hull was nearly identical to the two previous 5,500-ton classes, but internally the boiler rooms were laid out differently, which necessitated four stacks instead of the three on the previous classes. The four stacks became the easiest way to distinguish the Sendai class. Another difference was the raked bow given to *Jintsu* and *Sendai*. *Naka* did not possess this modification, but since its construction was delayed by the earthquake that struck Japan in 1923, it had a flared bow based on the heavy cruiser designs then under

Isuzu running trials in September 1944 after conversion into an antiaircraft cruiser. The location of the three Type 89 5-inch dual mounts can be clearly seen and some of the 25mm triple mounts have already been fitted. The aft Type 92 quadruple torpedo mount has been trained out. The No. 21 radar can be seen above the bridge and a No.13 set has been placed on the mainmast. (Yamato Museum)

construction. *Jintsu* received the same bow after it was repaired following a 1927 collision. The bridge was also slightly larger, with the hangar and flying platform in the forward superstructure also being retained. As on the Nagara class, there was no aft superstructure and the main deck covered the aft torpedo tubes.

### Sendai Class Construction

| Ship | Built at | Laid down | Launched | Completed |
|---|---|---|---|---|
| *Sendai* | Nagasaki, by Mitsubishi | 2/16/22 | 10/30/23 | 4/29/24 |
| *Jintsu* | Kobe, by Kawasaki | 10/4/22 | 12/8/23 | 7/31/25 |
| *Naka* | Yokohama Dock Company | 5/24/24 | 3/24/25 | 11/30/25 |

### Armament
The Sendai class was armed identically to units of the Nagara class.

### Service Modifications
In 1929, the forward flying platform was replaced with a catapult. This was subsequently removed between 1934 and 1937 and moved aft between 5.5-inch gun mounts No. 6 and 7. When the bridge was modified all three ships were fitted with a 13-foot rangefinder above the bridge. Before the start of the war, all three units were earmarked to receive Type 93 oxygen-propelled torpedoes since all three were flagships of destroyer squadrons. This was done March–May 1941 for all except *Sendai*. *Jintsu* and *Naka* received two quadruple Type 92 torpedo mounts aft. The forward twin mounts were removed and the area plated over and converted to crew quarters. Before the start of the war, all received two twin 25mm mounts.

All three ships were lost fairly early in the war during 1943 and early 1944. This limited the amount of modification the class received. In May 1943 *Sendai* had one 5.5-inch mount removed and two triple 25mm gun mounts installed. A No. 21 radar was added on top of the fire-control position on the foremast. *Sendai* was not further modified before its loss.

*Naka* received a similar modernization June 1942–April 1943. One 5.5-inch gun was removed and replaced by a Type 89 twin 5-inch mount. Two triple 25mm guns were also added and the 13mm quadruple mount in front of bridge was replaced with a twin 13mm mount. A No. 21 radar was added atop the foremast. The catapult was retained as on *Sendai*. No other modifications were

An excellent view of *Abukuma* on December 7, 1941, taken from one of the oilers of the Pearl Harbor Supply Force. *Abukuma* was the most modified Nagara-class cruiser before the war. It was provided with two quadruple Type 92 torpedo mounts (the port side mount is visible just aft of the first stack). The former position of the forward twin torpedo mount has been plated over as is evident in this view. The aircraft is a Type 94 reconnaissance seaplane. (Yamato Museum)

made before the ship was lost. The only modifications to *Jintsu* were the additions of two triple 25mm mounts in the area of the torpedo tubes aft.

| Sendai Class Modifications (final configuration when lost) | | | |
|---|---|---|---|
| Ship | *Sendai* | *Naka* | *Jintsu* |
| Torpedo tubes | 8 (4x2) | 8 (2x4) | 8 (2x4) |
| 5.5-inch guns | 6 | 6 | 7 |
| Type 89 twin 5 inch | 0 | 1 | 0 |
| Triple 25mm guns | 2 | 2 | 2 |
| Twin 25mm guns | 2 | 2 | 2 |
| Single 25mm guns | 0 | 0 | 0 |
| 13mm guns | 4 | 2 | 2 |
| Radar | No. 21 | No. 21 | None |

## Wartime Service

The prewar career of the Sendai class included the disastrous Special Great Maneuvers of August 1927. During these exercises, *Jintsu* rammed and sank a destroyer at 28 knots at night. *Naka* rammed a second destroyer, cutting off its stern. When war began, the Sendai class were the most modern of the 5,500-ton cruisers. As such, *Jintsu*, *Sendai*, and *Naka* began the war as flagships of Desron 2, 3, 4, respectively. In their capacity as destroyer squadron flagships, all saw heavy action during the first part of the war and all were committed to the savage battles in the Solomons. Accordingly, all were lost fairly early in the war.

*Sendai* began the war as flagship of Desron 3. It escorted Malaya invasion convoys into January 1942. On January 27, *Sendai* saw its first action when two destroyers (one British, one Australian) attempted to intercept the convoy *Sendai* and its destroyers were escorting. In the ensuing action (the battle off Endau), the British destroyer was sunk for no Japanese losses. After the fall of Singapore in February 1942, *Sendai* participated in the invasion of Sumatra in March.

After a refit, *Sendai* took part in the battle of Midway as an escort to the Main Body. When the Americans attacked Guadalcanal, Desron 3 was ordered to Truk. *Sendai* was soon active off Guadalcanal, conducting night-time resupply missions and shelling American-held Tulagi (once) and Guadalcanal (twice) during September. On the night of November 14–15, it was part of the Japanese attempt to shell Henderson Field. The mission failed with the loss of the battleship *Kirishima*, but *Sendai* was undamaged. In this night battle, it engaged American destroyers with torpedoes and gunfire.

From January 1943, *Sendai* was involved in constant patrol and escort duties in the northern Solomons, returning to Japan May–June 1943 for refit and limited modernization. Upon its return to action, it resumed escort duties in the Solomons. On November 1, American forces landed on Bougainville Island. The Japanese reacted immediately, sending a cruiser-destroyer force against the invasion. *Sendai* was part of the force gathered for this purpose. The action began early the next day. *Sendai* spotted the Americans and launched four torpedoes (all missed). In return it was smothered by 6-inch gunfire from four American light cruisers. Severe fires and flooding resulted, and

This close-up of the forward superstructure of *Abukuma* was taken on the morning of December 7, 1941. *Abukuma* was assigned to the Pearl Harbor Strike Force at the time. The white bundles around the superstructure are rolled-up canvas placed in key areas to provide a measure of protection against splinter damage. The superstructure reflects the changes from the 1938 modification with the 20-foot rangefinder on top of the bridge and the fire-control position on top of the tripod foremast. (*Ships of the World* magazine)

the ship was abandoned with the loss of 185 of its crew.

*Naka* began the war as flagship of Desron 4. This unit was assigned to escort convoys headed for Luzon. In this capacity, *Naka* was lightly damaged by American air attack on December 10. By late December it shifted to support the invasion of the Dutch East Indies. On January 24, the convoy *Naka* was escorting was attacked by four American destroyers. *Naka* had been drawn off by a Dutch submarine, and the four American ships proceeded to savage the convoy for no losses.

*Sendai* shown in the 1920s in its early configuration. The 33-foot take-off platform over the No. 2 5.5-inch gun mount and the aircraft hangar below the compass bridge are very evident. This platform could only be used by well-trained pilots and once launched, the aircraft could not recover aboard the cruiser. The entire arrangement was soon determined to be unworkable and the platform was removed and eventually replaced by a catapult mounted aft. (Naval History and Heritage Command)

In the battle of the Java Sea on February 27, 1942, both *Naka* and *Jintsu* were present as an Allied cruiser-destroyer force attempted to engage a Japanese invasion convoy. Though the battle was won by Japanese torpedoes, which sank three Dutch ships, all of the torpedoes fired by *Naka* (8) and *Jintsu* (12) missed their targets. However, the aircraft off these cruisers played an important role by tracking the Allied force during the night.

On March 31, while covering the occupation of Christmas Island, *Naka* was attacked by the American submarine *Seawolf*. One torpedo hit aft, which caused extensive damage. *Naka* was repaired at Singapore in May before returning to Japan. From April 1943, *Naka* operated in the Central Pacific in various escort and transport roles. In February 1944 it was caught in the major American carrier raid on Truk and on the 17th of that month it departed Truk to aid the torpedoed cruiser *Agano*. *Naka* came under immediate air attack. One torpedo hit forward and broke the hull in two. Only 210 of its crew were rescued.

*Jintsu* began the war as flagship of Desron 2, its first action escorting the Mindanao invasion force. In January 1942 it supported the invasion of the Dutch East Indies and participated in the battle of the Java Sea as mentioned above. In March *Jintsu* returned to Japan. In June it escorted the Midway Invasion Force and subsequently was committed to the increasingly savage battles around Guadalcanal. On August 25 *Jintsu* was subjected to air attack while escorting a convoy to the island. A 500-pound bomb hit forward, killed 24, wounded 27, and forced a return to Japan for repairs.

This 1927 photograph provides an overhead view of a Sendai-class cruiser. The seven 5.5-inch guns are evident as are the twin torpedo mounts located abreast the forward stack; the aft set of torpedo tubes have both been trained out and can be seen abaft the third stack. (*Ships of the World* magazine)

*Jintsu* returned to Truk in January 1943 to resume duties as flagship of Desron 2. It departed Rabaul on July 12 to conduct a reinforcement of Kolombangara in the Central Solomons. In the resulting battle of Kolombangara on July 13, 1943, the Japanese successfully employed their usual torpedo tactics, but this victory proved painful when *Jintsu* was hit by radar-controlled gunfire from three Allied light cruisers. The intense shellfire destroyed the bridge and the boiler rooms and *Jintsu* went dead in water. It was later hit by a destroyer-launched torpedo that broke the ship in half. *Jintsu* sank with heavy loss of life.

| Sendai Class Specifications | |
|---|---|
| Displacement | 7,609 tons full load (1925) |
| Dimensions | Length: 532ft overall / Beam: 46.5ft / Draft: 29ft |
| Speed | 35.25 knots |
| Range | 6,000nm at 14 knots (actual) |
| Crew | 37 officers and 413 enlisted personnel plus space for staff (5 officers and 22 enlisted) |

## Yubari Class
### Design and Construction

Construction of an experimental cruiser was authorized in the 8-4 Fleet Completion Program in 1917. However, no funds were immediately available and the design was not approved until October 1921 so the ship was not laid down until June 1922. The intent of the design was to create a ship that possessed a heavy armament and high speed on the smallest possible displacement. The design must be considered a success since it created a ship with the same speed, radius, and broadside armament on a much smaller displacement than the 5,500-ton cruisers.

This view of *Sendai* in 1937 near Shanghai, China shows the cruiser in its final configuration before going to war. The four stacks are easily discerned; this was the primary difference from the preceding Kuma and Nagara classes. Note the aft catapult fitted between 5.5-inch gun mounts No. 6 and 7. The crane mounted on the mainmast for aircraft handling can also be seen. (Naval History and Heritage Command)

The primary recognition feature of *Yubari* was its trunked stack. This was a design feature that would become common on subsequent Japanese cruisers. Other features on *Yubari* also proved successful and were incorporated into future designs. These included a bow curve, no more mixed-firing boilers, and, most importantly, the weight-saving feature of incorporating side and deck armor to increase the longitudinal strength of the hull. This meant the hull of *Yubari* was only 31 percent of displacement as opposed to 38 percent on the 5,500-ton cruisers. Even with these weight-saving measures and an overall smaller displacement, total armor on *Yubari* was almost twice that of the 5,500-ton ships.

Nevertheless, though the basic design principles were proven successful, the ship was overweight by 419 tons, or 14 percent of displacement. This was beyond what was considered normal by Japanese designers. The ship's design speed was 35.5 knots, achieved by eight boilers generating 57,900 SHP through three shafts.

| Yubari Class Construction | | | | |
|---|---|---|---|---|
| Ship | Built at | Laid down | Launched | Completed |
| *Yubari* | Sasebo NY | 6/5/22 | 3/5/23 | 7/31/23 |

### Armament

The main battery was the same broadside, six 5.5-inch guns, as mounted on the 5,500-ton cruisers. The difference was that the six guns on *Yubari* were mounted in a combination of two single mounts and two twin mounts. The twin mounts were actually gun houses protected by only a 10mm steel front plate. The tighter grouping of the mounts fore and aft also allowed for a higher rate of fire. Fire control provided by a director on the foremast and two 10-foot rangefinders placed on either side of the compass bridge.

The torpedo armament was two twin torpedo mounts with four reserve torpedoes. Antiaircraft protection was provided by a single 3.15-inch gun amidships and two 7.7mm machine guns.

### Service Modifications

In 1924, the height of the stack was raised by 6.5 feet to avoid the problem of gasses going into the bridge. In 1932–33, while in a yard, the 3.15-inch gun was removed and spray shields placed around the torpedo tubes. In 1935 two twin 13mm machine guns were fitted. These were replaced by twin 25mm mounts in 1940.

The ship received no modification (except the addition of a hydrophone set between August and October 1943) until its first major wartime refit period from December 1943 to March 1944. During this time, the ship's antiaircraft armament was greatly increased. The single 5.5-inch guns were removed; in the place of the forward mount, a Type 10 4.7-inch high-angle gun was fitted. The number of 25mm guns was increased to 25 with the addition of a triple mount replacing the aft 5.5-inch gun, two additional triple mounts fitted on the aft superstructure, two twin 25mm mounts fitted forward of the bridge, and eight single mounts. A No.22 radar replaced the searchlight atop the bridge and two depth charge rails were added aft. Speed was reduced to 32 knots.

**Wartime Service**

*Yubari* began the war as flagship of Destroyer Squadron 6 of the Fourth Fleet charged with protection of the Mandate Islands. For the first part of the war, *Yubari* saw action with *Tenryu* and *Tatsuta*, participating in the invasions of Wake, Rabaul/Kavieng, and Lae and Salamaua. When American carrier aircraft attacked the Lae/Salamaua invasion force, *Yubari* took near misses fore and aft that resulted in hull damage and small fires. These inflicted 14 dead and 30 wounded. It was forced to return to Truk for repairs, which were completed in mid-April. Its next operation was the invasion of Port Moresby when *Yubari* was assigned to the Port Moresby Attack Force (the invasion convoy). *Yubari* returned to Truk after the failure of the operation. Following a short refit in Japan from May 23–June 15, it returned to Truk on June 23.

The highlight of *Yubari's* career was its participation in the battle of Savo Island following the American invasion of Guadalcanal. It took a dud hit early in the action, but one of its torpedoes hit the American heavy cruiser *Vincennes*, which later sank. *Yubari* then proceeded to pound the destroyer *Ralph Talbot*, which escaped by moving into a rain squall. In total, *Yubari* fired 96 5.5-inch shells and four torpedoes during the battle.

*Yubari* missed the rest of the Guadalcanal campaign after it was assigned to escort convoys to and from Truk into 1943. On April 1, 1943, it arrived at

**D** **CRUISER *YUBARI* DEPARTING SIMPSON HARBOR, RABAUL**

On August 7, 1942 American Marines landed on the island of Guadalcanal. By that morning, Vice Admiral Mikawa Gunichi, commander of the 8th Fleet based at Rabaul, decided to contest the American invasion with a night surface attack with all available forces. By afternoon, the scratch Japanese force of seven cruisers and a destroyer departed Rabaul en route to Guadalcanal. This view shows *Yubari* departing Simpson Harbor. The ship presents a compact appearance with a single trunked stack and a symmetrical main battery with the twin 5.5-inch gun houses mounted in a superfiring position over the single 5.5-inch mounts. Despite Mikawa's apprehension about including a unit as old as *Yubari*, on the night of August 9, it performed well in the battle of Savo Island.

This prewar view of *Yubari* shows the cruiser before it was lightly modernized before the Pacific War. Assigned to largely secondary duties, *Yubari* had a busy wartime career before being sunk in 1944. (Naval History and Heritage Command)

Rabaul for front-line duties but was promptly damaged by a mine on July 5 that forced it home for repairs. It returned to Rabaul by November 1943 only to be ordered back to Japan in December to augment its antiaircraft armament.

After completion of this refit, *Yubari* was ordered to escort convoys in the Central Pacific. It embarked 365 army troops and supplies at the Palau Islands and headed to Sonsorol Island to the southwest. After disembarking the troops and their supplies, the cruiser was struck by a single torpedo from the submarine *Bluegill* on April 27, 1944. The single hit flooded two boiler rooms and the flooding could not be stopped. Early on the next day, *Yubari* sank with a loss of 19 crewmen.

| Yubari Class Specifications | |
| --- | --- |
| Displacement | 4,447 tons full load (August 1923) |
| Dimensions | Length: 457.5ft overall / Beam 39.5ft / Draft: 23.75ft |
| Speed | 35.5 knots |
| Range | 3,310nm at 14 knots (actual) |
| Crew | 328 officers and enlisted personnel |

## Agano Class
### Design and Construction
The 5,500-ton cruisers were designed specifically with duties as destroyer squadron flagships in mind. However, by the late 1930s these ships were increasingly unsuited for their assigned role. In the view of the Imperial Navy, these shortcomings were significant and included just about everything that was worth mentioning. The 5,500-ton cruisers were now slower than the newest Japanese destroyers, possessed less endurance, and, perhaps most importantly, did not possess any advantage in firepower. The old cruisers could present a broadside of six 5.5-inch guns and four torpedo tubes. The newer destroyers had a broadside of six 5-inch guns (which had a greater rate of fire) and up to nine torpedo tubes. The older ships were also viewed as deficient in their scouting capabilities since they carried only a single floatplane – the Japanese thought that two were necessary.

As long as the Japanese were bound by the London Naval Treaty, their cruiser construction was limited. This restriction was lifted when Japan announced its intention to leave the treaty. The Naval General Staff planned to build 13 6,000 ton cruisers, six for destroyer squadrons, and seven for submarine squadrons. These were to be built from 1939 to 1945. The final decision on the program was made in September 1938. Four destroyer squadron flagships were to be ordered (these became the Agano class) and two submarine squadron flagships (these became the Oyodo class). This proposal was approved in March 1939 as part of the Fourth Replenishment Program.

The design of the new class was not finalized until October 1939. The final result was a beautiful ship with a graceful deck line in which the sheer was less pronounced from amidships to the stern than other 1930s Japanese cruiser designs. The design appeared uncluttered, with a small bridge structure, a single stack, and three main

*Yubari* in about 1925 after the stack was raised to address the problem of gases going into the bridge. This view clearly shows its compact appearance and the arrangement of its main battery of six 5.5-inch guns in four gun houses. The two double torpedo mounts are also discernable amidships. (Naval History and Heritage Command)

turrets. A significant portion of the topside space was devoted to aircraft handling facilities, which included a catapult, a platform for two aircraft, and an aircraft crane mounted on the mainmast aft. Overall, the ship gave an impression of being underarmed, which it was.

Armor was improved over previous light cruisers, but was still limited. The design specifications called for protection of the magazine and machinery spaces against 6-inch and 5-inch gunfire. The side belt incorporated 60mm of armor, which extended beyond the machinery spaces. Protection of the forward and aft magazines was supplemented by a 55mm belt of steel. Deck armor was only 20mm over machinery and magazine spaces; total armor for the entire ship was just 656 tons. The small beam prevented any anti-torpedo protection from being provided, but internal compartmentation was extensive.

The class was designed to attain 35 knots. This required a total of 100,000 SHP generated by four sets of turbines. Six boilers were placed in five boiler rooms. On trials, both *Agano* and *Yahagi* slightly exceeded their design speed.

**Agano Class Construction**

| Ship | Built at | Laid down | Launched | Completed |
|------|----------|-----------|----------|-----------|
| *Agano* | Sasebo NY | 6/18/40 | 10/22/41 | 10/31/42 |
| *Noshiro* | Yokosuka NY | 9/4/41 | 7/19/42 | 6/30/43 |
| *Yahagi* | Sasebo NY | 11/11/41 | 10/25/42 | 12/29/43 |
| *Sakawa* | Sasebo NY | 11/21/42 | 4/9/44 | 11/30/44 |

## Armament

The new cruiser's main battery was six Type 41 6-inch/50 guns. These dated from 1912 and had been in service as secondary guns on Japanese battleships. In the Agano class, they were mounted in three twin turrets. Antiaircraft armament featured the new 3.15-inch high-angle gun designed specifically for the Agano class. However, only two twin mounts were fitted. Light antiaircraft armament was limited to two triple 25mm mounts in front of bridge and two twin 13mm mounts near the mainmast.

The Agano class did possess a major increase in torpedo firepower. Two quadruple Type 92 torpedo mounts were fitted below the aircraft platform. These were on the centerline and were rotatable, so could fire in either direction. Eight reserve torpedoes were also carried, which could be reloaded in 20-30 minutes. All four ships were completed with two depth charge racks on the stern. The ships were also provided with a hydrophone for passive detection and a sonar for active detection of submarines.

## Service Modifications

Wartime modifications focused on improving the radar and light antiaircraft fit. Since the last two ships were finished late into the war, both incorporated improvements already made on the two ships in service.

*Agano* was completed without radar, but a No. 21 set was added in June 1943. This was placed on the front of the rangefinder tower, giving the radar a 360-degree rotation. The other ships were completed with a No. 21 radar. In July 1944 *Noshiro* and *Yahagi* were fitted with a No. 22 and a

A starboard beam view of *Agano* in 1943 showing its primary design features. The three twin 6.1-inch gun turrets are visible as is the small bridge and the prominent stack. The two aircraft are Type 0 reconnaissance seaplanes (E13A1, also known by their Allied codename "Jake"). One of the Type 92 quadruple torpedo launchers can be seen under the catapult; the other was located under the aircraft platform but is not visible. (Yamato Museum)

*Noshiro* running trials in June 1943. The view shows the uncluttered design to full effect. Unlike the lead ship in the class, *Agano*, *Noshiro* was completed with a No. 21 radar on the front of the fire-control tower. (Yamato Museum)

This photograph taken by USS *Yorktown* (CV-10) aircraft shows *Yahagi* on its final sortie after being hit by a torpedo. The ship is bleeding oil and is dead in the water, making it helpless against subsequent attacks. (Naval History and Heritage Command)

No. 13 radar. The No. 22 set was fitted on both sides of the bridge at the level of the antiaircraft command platform. The large No. 13 set was fitted on the trailing side of the foremast. *Sakawa* was completed with all three radars in place.

*Agano* received little modification before being sunk. When it received its radar in June 1943, it also received two triple and two twin 25mm mounts. *Noshiro* received additional 25mm guns to bring its total to 32 (eight triple and eight single) in its early 1944 repair and refit period. *Yahagi* was also augmented to 32 25mm guns before leaving Japan for combat duty. After the battle of the Philippine Sea both *Noshiro* and *Yahagi* received additional radar (No. 22 and 13) and had their light antiaircraft fit increased to 48 25mm guns (10 triple, 18 single with another four relocatable guns). *Yahagi's* final modifications in November–December 1944 increased the 25mm total to 58 – 10 triple and 28 single. The table below gives the final 25mm gun configuration for each ship in the class.

| Agano Class 25mm Gun Fit | | | | |
|---|---|---|---|---|
| Ship | Triple Mounts | Twin Mounts | Single Mounts | Total |
| *Agano* | 4 | 2 | 0 | 16 |
| *Noshiro* | 10 | 0 | 18 | 48 |
| *Yahagi* | 10 | 0 | 28 | 58 |
| *Sakawa* | 10 | 0 | 42 | 72 |

## Wartime Service

*Agano* was the first ship to reach completion but was not assigned to an operational unit until November 1942. At this time it assumed flagship duties for Desron 10, relieving *Nagara*. After arriving at Truk in December, it was in action later in the month, participating in the seizure of Madang and Wewak on New Guinea. In January, it covered the evacuation of Guadalcanal.

*Agano's* first real action was in the battle of Empress Augusta Bay on November 2. Though undamaged in the battle, the combat debut of the new class of cruiser was not auspicious. It contributed nothing to the battle, which resulted in a Japanese defeat and the sinking of *Sendai* as described earlier. *Noshiro* entered service in August 1943 as flagship of Desron 2, replacing the sunken *Jintsu*. On November 3 it was ordered to depart Truk with seven heavy cruisers to complete the destruction of the American forces off Bougainville. After arriving at Rabaul two days later, the cruiser force was attacked by American carrier aircraft. Both *Agano* and *Noshiro* were caught in port but neither suffered serious damage. However, when the Americans returned on November 11, *Noshiro* again incurred only slight damage but

**E** ***YAHAGI* UNDER ATTACK BY US CARRIER AIRCRAFT IN APRIL 1945**

*Yahagi* and eight destroyers were detailed to escort the superbattleship *Yamato* in Operation *Ten-Ichi-Go* to attack the American invasion force off Okinawa. After departing on April 6, the force was attacked by American carrier aircraft just after noon the next day. *Yahagi* was hit in the first wave of attackers with an air-launched torpedo that caused it to lose power and go dead in the water. Subsequent waves pounded the cruiser to destruction with as many as six more torpedoes and 12 bombs. Of its crew of some 1,000 men, 445 were lost. Note the modifications to the ship including a total of 58 25mm guns and a full suite of radar.

Agano was hit by an aircraft torpedo outside Rabaul harbor. The hit sheered the stern section away, but flooding was limited and the ship reached the safety of Rabaul.

This port beam view of *Yahagi* was taken in December 1943 only a few days before commissioning. The clear photograph shows the beauty of the design and the several differences of the third ship of the class upon completion. The catapult is a smaller 64-foot version and the Type 94 high-angle directors have been moved forward to the area of the stack. The ship's antiaircraft suite was also heavier upon completion. (Yamato Museum)

The next day *Agano* departed Rabaul for Truk. It was attacked by the submarine *Scamp*, which hit the cruiser with one of a six-torpedo broadside. The hit flooded all boiler rooms, and *Noshiro* was forced to take *Agano* in tow. On November 16 *Agano* reached Truk under tow; it subsequently departed on February 15 for Japan. It was struck by the submarine *Skate* north of Truk the next day with by two torpedoes. The damage was severe and resulted in a loss of power and progressive flooding. *Agano* sank early on February 17.

*Noshiro* continued operations out of Truk. On January 1, 1944, it was attacked by carrier aircraft north of Kavieng. One direct hit destroyed its No. 2 turret and several near misses caused severe hull damage. *Noshiro* was forced to return to Japan for repairs. After the completion of the repairs, *Noshiro* arrived at Lingga in April. *Yahagi* also arrived at Lingga in February as flagship of Desron 10. Both ships took part in the battle of the Philippine Sea and were undamaged. After a short refit in Japan, they returned to Lingga in July.

As part of Force A, *Noshiro* and *Yahagi* departed Lingga on October 18 as the Imperial Navy committed all its remaining heavy units to meet the American invasion of the Philippines. In the October 25 battle of Samar, *Yahagi* led six destroyers of Desron 10 and *Noshiro* led nine destroyers of Desron 2. In the battle, *Yahagi* launched seven torpedoes at American escort carriers without result. It was hit by a single 5-inch destroyer shell. It underwent numerous air attacks during the battle and after, but suffered only near misses. However, losses primarily to strafing totaled 80 crewmen killed or wounded.

*Noshiro* also survived battle with a single 5-inch hit, but did take several damaging near misses from escort carrier aircraft. It engaged two escort carriers with gunfire and claimed several hits. The next day, October 26, while withdrawing, it was attacked by carrier aircraft and hit by a single torpedo, which resulted in flooding, loss of power, and a severe list. A second torpedo hit that evening sank the ship with a loss of all but 328 of its crew.

*Yahagi* returned to Japan in November. When the Americans invaded Okinawa, it was assigned to the Surface Special Attack Force as part of the *Ten-Ichi-Go* (Heaven Number One) Operation. It departed on April 6 en route to Okinawa with the superbattleship *Yamato* and eight destroyers in the Imperial Navy's last major operation. The following day this small force came under intensive air attack. Early in the action, an air-launched torpedo hit *Yahagi*. The hit destroyed the engine rooms and brought the ship dead in the water. The cruiser was helpless at this point. It was struck by another six torpedoes and at least 12 bombs and sank with the loss of 446 crewmen.

*Sakawa* as it appeared in November 1944 shortly before commissioning. Upon completion, *Sakawa* incorporated the radar and antiaircraft gun additions already made to the other ships in the class. In addition, the arrangement of the aircraft platform was different. (Yamato Museum)

*Sakawa* was assigned to Desron 11 in December 1944. Due to fuel shortages, it was unable to take part in the *Ten-Ichi-Go* Operation. *Sakawa* remained in the Inland Sea on training duties until July 1945. It was surrendered intact and

employed as a repatriation transport until February 1946. Subsequently, the cruiser was used as a target in the atomic tests at Bikini Atoll. In the July 1 test, it was badly damaged by an air burst and sank the next day.

| Agano Class Specifications | |
| --- | --- |
| Displacement | 8,534 tons full load |
| Dimensions | Length: 572.35ft overall / Beam: 49.9ft 1 / Draft: 8.5ft |
| Speed | 35 knots |
| Range | 6,000nm at 18 knots |
| Crew | 51 officers and 649 enlisted personnel as designed; *Sakawa* had 55 officers and 750 enlisted when completed |

## Oyodo Class
### Design and Construction
As mentioned in the previous section on the Agano class, the Imperial Navy also had a requirement for a cruiser designed to act as the flagship for a submarine squadron. This requirement was linked to the Japanese concept of submarine warfare in which long-range cruiser submarines would concentrate to attack enemy fleet units at extended ranges. The flagship cruiser was needed to provide targeting for the submarines and to coordinate their operations. To do this, it needed aircraft for scouting purposes, high speed and great endurance, and sufficient armament to combat enemy light units. Communications and accommodations for the embarked staff were also important. There were never enough cruisers to cover the submarine squadron flagship requirement and the 5,500-ton units occasionally assigned to act in this role were unsatisfactory.

In the 1930s, the Imperial Navy had a requirement for seven flagship cruisers for its seven submarine squadrons. Originally it was thought that the new class of cruisers being designed to replace the 5,500-ton units could support both destroyer and submarine flagship duties, but this was soon proven to be wishful thinking. Several different designs were created in 1938 until a definitive design for "Cruisers C" was completed in October. The same appropriations funding that provided for the four new Agano-class units approved in March 1938 also included funding for two new submarine flagship cruisers. Construction of the first ship was delayed, and this meant a subsequent delay in the start of the construction of the second, which ultimately resulted in its cancellation.

The design of the new class, named after the first ship laid down, *Oyodo*, was identical to that of the Agano class in regards to its hull lines and forward superstructure. The armament differed as described below, but the most important difference between the two cruiser designs was the aircraft-handling facilities. The original design for the Oyodo class called for a special 144-foot catapult fitted aft on the ship's centerline. Forward of the catapult was a hangar capable of storing four aircraft, with deck stowage for another two. These were of a new design with the high speed and long range required for scouting duties.

The propulsion system was more powerful than the Agano class. Four sets of turbines generated 110,000 SHP, which translated to a maximum speed of 35 knots. The radius of action as designed was 8,700nm at 18 knots; however, in service, it proved to be 10,000nm at 18 knots

Protection was designed to withstand 6-inch shellfire or a 550-pound bomb dropped from 9,900 feet. The side belt armor was 60mm, supplemented by an armored box covering the forward magazines and the machinery spaces amidships with an additional 30–75mm of armor. The main deck was covered by 30mm of armor over the machinery spaces and 50mm over the magazines. No anti-torpedo defenses were provided.

This is another view of *Sakawa* postwar in the process of being disarmed. The number 1 denotes the No. 22 radars and the number 2 denotes the No. 21 radar. The two forward 6-inch gun turrets are evident; note the rangefinder fitted on top of the second turret. (Naval History and Heritage Command)

| Oyodo Class Construction | | | | |
|---|---|---|---|---|
| Ship | Built at | Laid down | Launched | Completed |
| *Oyodo* | Kure NY | 2/14/41 | 4/2/42 | 2/28/43 |

### Armament

The main battery was positioned forward since the after part of the ship was devoted solely to aircraft-handling facilities. Two triple 6.1-inch turrets were used: these were turrets removed from the Mogami class cruisers when they were converted to heavy cruisers. Long-range antiaircraft protection was provided by four new 3.9-inch twin high-angle mounts. Short range antiaircraft protection, as completed, was six triple 25mm mounts. No torpedo mounts were fitted, making this the only Japanese light cruiser not to carry torpedoes when completed.

### Service Modifications

The ship was completed without radar. In April 1943 a No. 21 radar was installed on the rangefinder tower. In March 1944 *Oyodo* was modified from its role as a submarine squadron flagship to that of Combined Fleet flagship. The hangar was converted into space for an office and living quarters for the staff. The large catapult was replaced with a smaller 62-foot model. After this modification, only two seaplanes could be carried. Six additional triple and 11 single 25mm gun mounts were also added, bringing the total to 47.

In early October 1944 six more single 25mm mounts were added. A No. 13 radar was added on the mast above the hangar and two No. 22 radars were placed on the bridge wings. In late October, four more single 25mm guns were added for a final total of 57 – 12 triple and 21 single mounts.

### Wartime Service

After the ship was commissioned in February 1943, it was immediately apparent that the role it was designed for no longer existed. It was assigned to the Imperial Navy's carrier fleet since *Oyodo's* large cruising radius and decent antiaircraft capability made it suited to act as a carrier escort. Its first mission beyond home waters was a transport mission to Rabaul in July 1943. Following this, it remained at Truk for the next seven months. On January 1, 1944, on a mission to Kavieng, *Oyodo* came under carrier air attack but suffered only light damage. It returned to Japan in March 1944 for conversion. After modification, *Oyodo* moved to Tokyo Bay to assume its new role as Combined Fleet flagship. In late September the Combined Fleet moved ashore so *Oyodo* returned to fleet service and was again assigned to the carrier force.

### THE WAR-BUILT CRUISERS

The top and middle profiles show the *Agano* as it was completed. This class was the ultimate development of Japanese light cruisers. The ship gives a graceful and speedy appearance, though also seems to be underarmed and weakly armored. The main battery of three 6-inch twin guns is evident; the torpedo launchers can be seen under the aircraft platform and the catapult. Much of the ship is devoted to the aircraft-handling facilities. The bottom profile shows *Oyodo*, a one-of-a-kind light cruiser built for fleet command and control. This is the ship's configuration in October 1944 when it participated in the battle of Leyte Gulf. The similarity to the Agano class is obvious with the same bridge design, trunked stack, and graceful hull line. However, the ship lacks any torpedo armament, has triple 6.1-inch turrets mounted forward, and is fitted with two 3.9-inch antiaircraft guns amidships. The ship is shown with the smaller catapult fitted earlier in 1944 and a profusion of 25mm gun mounts.

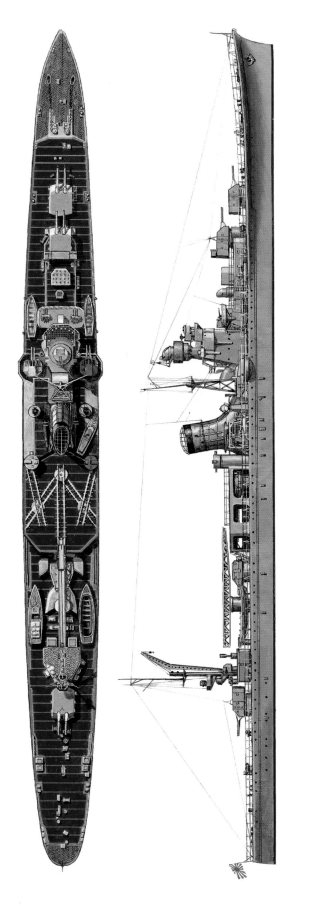
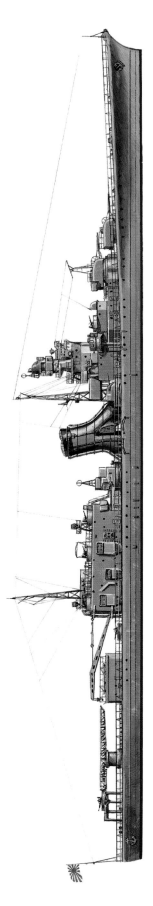

*Oyodo* departed with the carrier force on October 20 for the battle of Leyte Gulf. During the heavy air strikes launched by the Americans against the Imperial Navy's last carrier force, *Oyodo* was damaged by two rockets and a near miss from a bomb that killed eight and wounded 12. After Leyte Gulf, *Oyodo* was sent to Lingga. From there it took part in the San Jose intrusion operation against the American beachhead on Mindoro on December 26. This was a totally ineffective undertaking during which *Oyodo* was hit by two bombs (one a dud) and fired 98 main battery rounds. It was repaired at Singapore.

In February 1945 *Oyodo* was ordered to return to Japan with the battleships *Ise* and *Hyuga*. All three ships, as well as their three escorting destroyers, were loaded with oil, strategic materials, and key personnel for the transit north. Despite the efforts of as many as 25 American submarines, the force arrived safely in Japan on February 20.

During the last months of the war, *Oyodo*, like the rest of the Imperial Fleet, was hunted down in home waters by American carrier strikes. On March 19 at Kure, it was struck by three bombs. By April, it was repaired and made combat-ready. On July 24, *Oyodo* was hit by five bombs but this damage was contained by the crew. The next attack on July 28 was fatal. At least four bomb hits and many near misses to starboard opened the plates to the forward engine room and an aft boiler room, which resulted in flooding and the ship's capsizing in only 25 feet of water. The ship was raised in 1947 and scrapped by August 1948.

| Oyodo Class Specifications | |
|---|---|
| Displacement | 11,433 tons full load (February 1943) |
| Dimensions | Length: 629.75ft overall / Beam: 54.5ft / Draft: 19.5ft |
| Speed | 35 knots |
| Range | 10,315nm at 18 knots |
| Crew | 53 officers and 723 enlisted personnel |

## Katori Class
### Design and Construction

The three units of the Katori class were not intended to be combatant ships. The Japanese classified them as "training cruisers," although this was not actually a subcategory of cruisers, but a separate class meant for training ships. The genesis of the class began in 1937 when the Naval General Staff decided it needed a new class of training ships for long-range training cruises of midshipman. Originally it was planned to modify three aging Kuma class units, but after Japan renounced the naval treaties, this plan was dropped.

The new class of ship emphasized accommodations and training facilities. Accordingly, much of the equipment found on other Imperial Navy ships was fitted, including an array of different weapons, fire control and navigational equipment and both steam turbine and diesel engines. The bridge was designed to accommodate a large number of midshipmen.

Overall, living quarters were generous by Imperial Navy standards. Given this, they were well suited to act as fleet flagships during wartime. The first two ships were authorized in 1937 and the third in 1938. A planned fourth ship was cancelled in 1941.

The basic design of the class reflected its mission. They gave an austere appearance with a basic forward superstructure, a single stack, and a small aft superstructure. Since speed was not a design requirement, the length-to-beam ratio was only 8.15, which gave the ships a stubby appearance. The combined turbine and diesel propulsion system was sufficient for only 8,000 SHP, but this met the design speed of 18 knots.

*Oyodo* approaching the crippled carrier *Zuikaku* on October 25, 1944 during the battle of Leyte Gulf to remove Vice Admiral Ozawa and his staff. A careful examination of the mainmast shows a No. 13 air search radar, but other late war modifications given to the ship are not visible. (Naval History and Heritage Command)

| Katori Class Construction | | | | |
|---|---|---|---|---|
| Ship | Built at | Laid down | Launched | Completed |
| *Katori* | Yokohama, by Mitsubishi | 8/24/38 | 6/17/39 | 4/20/40 |
| *Kashima* | Yokohama, by Mitsubishi | 10/6/38 | 9/25/39 | 5/31/40 |
| *Kashii* | Yokohama, by Mitsubishi | 10/4/39 | 10/15/40 | 7/15/41 |

## Armament

The original armament of the Katori class included four 5.5-inch guns in twin gun houses mounted fore and aft, and a Type 89 twin 5-inch mount aft. Four 2-inch saluting guns were fitted on *Katori* and *Kashima*, but these were removed in August 1942. Two were fitted on *Kashii* upon its completion. *Katori* and *Kashima* were give two twin 25mm mounts, which were placed abreast the bridge. When the saluting guns were removed, two additional twin 25mm guns were added. *Kashii* was completed with four twin 25mm guns. Two twin torpedo mounts were fitted abreast the funnel. No torpedo reloads were carried. A catapult was also fitted abaft the stack with room for a single floatplane.

## Service Modifications

*Katori* received no modifications with the exception of the addition of two twin 25mm mounts already mentioned. Two ships underwent conversion into antisubmarine sweeping ships. The first to be converted was *Kashii*, between March and April 1944. This work included the removal of the torpedo mounts, which were replaced by two Type 89 twin 5-inch mounts, and the addition of four triple 25mm mounts for a total of 20 25mm guns (four triple, four twin). A No. 21 radar was fitted on the foremast. To equip it in its new role as a submarine hunter, hydrophones and sonar were installed in addition to two depth charge racks and four throwers on the quarterdeck, with 300 depth charges that were stowed in a concrete-lined magazine created from the former headquarters spaces. In June–July 1944 *Kashii* received another ten single 25mm guns and eight single 13mm machine guns. Also at this time, a No. 22 radar replaced the No. 21 on the foremast.

*Kashima* received similar modifications in December 1944–January 1945. In addition to the works described above, it received ten single 25mm mounts, and a No. 22 radar was fitted on

Training cruiser *Katori* as it appeared in April 1940. The three rows of scuttles along the hull and the saluting guns forward of the bridge hint at its primary mission. The catapult (covered in brown canvas) is located amidships and the white canvas covered object located abreast the single stack is a dual torpedo mount. (Yamato Museum)

the foremast. Final modifications in February 1945 included adding a No. 13 radar on the foremast and eight more single 25mm guns.

## Wartime Service

*Katori*, commissioned in April 1940, conducted only a single training cruise before it was pulled from training duties to be converted to a fleet flagship. It was originally assigned as flagship of Subron 1 in November 1940, but then was designated flagship of the Sixth (submarine) Fleet in May 1941. On February 1, 1942, while at Kwajalein, it was attacked by American carrier aircraft but was only slightly damaged. After repairs in Japan, it returned to Truk in April. Aside from two short refit periods in Japan, it remained in the central Pacific, mostly at Truk, as Sixth Fleet flagship, until February 1944. At this time it was transferred to the General Escort Command and was ordered home for conversion into an antisubmarine ship. Unfortunately for *Katori*, its departure from Truk coincided with the arrival of the American carrier force then raiding Truk. On February 17 it was hit by an aircraft torpedo but made emergency repairs and was proceeding slowly until it encountered an American cruiser force making a sweep around the atoll. *Katori* was sunk by gunfire 40nm northwest of Truk.

*Kashima* was the only training cruiser to survive the war. With *Katori*, it completed its only training cruise in 1940 before being pulled for conversion into a flagship. It was assigned flagship of *Sentai* 18 on November 15 and later as flagship of the Fourth Fleet on December 1, 1941. In this capacity, it spent most of its time at Truk. It did conduct two refits in Japan, but by November 1943 was ordered to turn over Fourth Fleet flagship duties to *Nagara* and return to Japan to resume training duties.

From December 1943 until December 1944, *Kashima* conducted training cruises for midshipmen in the Inland Sea. During this time it was also employed in a series of emergency transport runs. In December 1944 it began conversion into an antisubmarine sweeping ship. This was completed in late January 1945. During its brief tenure as a submarine hunter, *Kashima* operated in the East China Sea and in the Sea of Japan, without success. It was surrendered after Japan's defeat and was used as a repatriation transport until November 1946 after which it was scrapped.

**THE TENRYU AND KATORI CLASSES**

The top profile shows *Tenryu*, the first modern Japanese light cruiser. The ship's main armament of four 5.5-inch guns and two triple torpedo mounts is evident. The middle profile is *Katori* in its prewar training cruiser configuration. The ship presents an austere appearance with a single stack, a catapult amidships, and twin 5.5-inch gun houses fore and aft. The large bridge structure is attributable to its training function. The bottom view is *Kashii* in 1945 just before its loss after it had been converted to an antisubmarine cruiser. Modifications include the removal of the amidships torpedo mounts and the addition of many 25mm guns throughout the ship and the addition of depth charge handling equipment on the quarterdeck. Note the addition of a No. 22 radar on the foremast.

*Kashii* did not enter service until July 1941. It was immediately based in French Indochina from which it provided escort for Malaya invasion convoys at the start of war. *Kashii* transitioned in February to escort invasion forces bound for Sumatra. After the surrender of the Dutch East Indies, it remained in the southwest area operating out of Singapore. As was the case for *Kashima*, *Kashii* returned to Japan in December 1943 to resume training of midshipmen. This was short-lived. In March, *Kashii* was subordinated to the General Escort Command after conversion into an antisubmarine sweeping ship. This conversion was completed in a month in Kure Navy Yard.

In its new career as a submarine hunter, *Kashii* was assigned as flagship of No. 1 Surface Escort Division responsible for running convoys between Japan and Singapore. On its fifth return trip from Singapore, *Kashii*, now flagship of the No. 101 Escort Squadron, encountered an American carrier task force then rampaging through the South China Sea. The ten-ship convoy *Kashii* was escorting was annihilated and the ship took a torpedo amidships and two bomb hits, one of which penetrated the depth charge magazine. Only 19 of its crew survived.

| Katori Class Specifications | |
|---|---|
| Displacement | 5,890 tons standard; 6,720 tons full load |
| Dimensions | Length: 437.9ft overall / Beam: 54.5ft / Draft: 3.75ft |
| Speed | 18 knots |
| Range | 9,900nm at 12 knots |
| Crew | 315 officers and enlisted personnel in ship's company with space for 275 midshipmen |

## ANALYSIS AND CONCLUSION

As designed, the Imperial Navy's light cruisers were underarmed compared to their foreign counterparts, carried almost no antiaircraft protection, and possessed a mediocre torpedo armament. Most of all, with the progression of larger, faster Japanese destroyer designs in the late 1920s and 1930s, they were barely capable of acting in their design capacity as destroyer squadron flagships. The Japanese were aware of this situation, and as soon as they were out from under naval treaty limitations, they built new destroyer squadron flagships with heavier armament, greater speed, and greater scouting capabilities. Overall, when discussing the Imperial Navy's 5,500-ton designs, they must be considered marginally successful given the undoubted success of the Imperial Navy's light forces, which the light cruisers were responsible for leading.

In addition to their role as destroyer squadron flagships, Japanese light cruisers were employed in many other roles. They enjoyed no great success in any of these, but performed all adequately. However, as the war progressed, and American air and naval power penetrated deeply into Japanese-held areas, the weaknesses of the Imperial Navy's light cruisers became obvious. Of the 22 non-training light cruisers, only two survived. The primary agent of loss for each ship is shown in the table below.

| Losses of IJN Light Cruisers by Primary Cause | | |
|---|---|---|
| Surface Action | 2 | *Sendai, Jintsu* |
| Air Attack | 7 | *Kiso, Yura, Kinu, Abukuma, Noshiro, Yahagi, Oyodo* |
| Submarine Attack | 11 | *Tenryu, Tatsuta, Kuma, Tama, Oi, Nagara, Isuzu, Natori, Naka, Yubari, Agano* |

The general conclusion from the table above is that when Japanese light cruisers were employed against Allied surface forces, they generally performed well. However, throughout the war they proved vulnerable to air attack. Unable to protect themselves and unable to take a great degree of damage, seven were sunk, and almost every ship damaged at least once, by air attack. Most apparent is their vulnerability to submarine attack. Since most light cruisers were not considered major fleet units, they were assigned secondary missions. In this capacity, they were not given adequate antisubmarine protection, and the results were evident. Japanese light cruisers did not possess dedicated anti-torpedo defenses, so when torpedoed, one or two torpedoes were adequate to sink the ship.

The utility of the last generation of light cruisers, the Agano and Oyodo classes, must be questioned. The Japanese notion of using light cruisers to lead destroyers and submarines was deeply ingrained, and the design of the last light cruisers built reflected this specialized role. What resulted in the case of the Agano class was a beautiful ship, but one that was outclassed by foreign light cruiser designs in the areas of firepower and protection. The concept of using light cruisers as an operational flagship for submarine squadrons was never more than a fantasy, so this made the *Oyodo* nothing more than a white elephant. Had the Mogami and Tone classes, the missing generation of Japanese light cruisers, not been converted into heavy cruisers, they would have been remembered as tough, well-armed light cruisers. With their conversion, all that was left in the Imperial Navy's light cruiser ranks was a collection of overaged, underarmed, and marginally protected ships suited only for specialized roles.

This photo shows a Nagara-class cruiser under attack from aircraft from carrier USS *Lexington* on December 4, 1943. The attack took place off Kwajalein. Based on the ship's characteristics, this is probably *Nagara*, though the possibility exists it could be *Isuzu*, since both were in the area on this date. Despite the fire and smoke caused by the burning floatplane, *Nagara* was only lightly damaged. (Naval History and Heritage Command)

# BIBLIOGRAPHY

Campbell, John, *Naval Weapons of World War Two*, Naval Institute Press, Annapolis, Maryland (1985)

Evans, David C. and Peattie, Mark R., *Kaigun*, Naval Institute Press, Annapolis, Maryland (1997)

Jentschura, Hansgeorg, Jung, Dieter and Mickel, Peter, *Warships of the Imperial Japanese Navy 1869-1945*, Naval Institute Press, Annapolis, Maryland (1977)

Lacroix, Eric and Wells II, Linton, *Japanese Cruisers of the Pacific War*, Naval Institute Press, Annapolis, Maryland (1997)

O'Hara, Vincent P., *The U.S. Navy Against the Axis*, Naval Institute Press, Annapolis, Maryland (2006)

Stille, Mark, *USN Cruiser vs IJN Cruiser*, Osprey, Oxford (2009)

Watts, Anthony J. and Gordon, Brian G., *The Imperial Japanese Navy*, Macdonald, London (1971)

Whitley, M.J., *Cruisers of World War Two*, Naval Institute Press, Annapolis, Maryland (1995)

www.combinedfleet.com

# INDEX

Note: letters in **bold** refer to plates and illustrations.